FROM EAST TO WEST

In his most audacious and radical book to date, Roy Bhaskar develops his existing philosophy of dialectical critical realism into a philosophy of and for universal self-realisation, which he also terms a transcendental dialectical critical realism. A general theoretical introduction establishes the existence of God as the fundamental categorial structure of the world and unconditional love as the cement of the universe.

This system of thought is followed by a narrative novella designed to render plausible the ideas of reincarnation, *karma* and *moksha* or liberation and to support an ethic of engaged but unattached activity in the world, ultimately oriented to universal self-realisation in the becoming of what *From East to West* argues *we already essentially* (but only partially, i.e. not only) *are*, namely free or enlightened. To realise this, Bhaskar argues, we have to shed both the illusion that we are not essentially free and Godlike, and the constraining determinations (constituting an objective world of illusion, duality and alienation) which that illusion grounds.

A radical resynthesis of aspects of Western and Eastern thought, this book is also a major new development in critical realism. *From East to West* is bound to stimulate debate in ontology, epistemology, ethics, political philosophy and the philosophy of (comparative) religion.

Roy Bhaskar is the originator of the philosophy of critical realism, and the author of many acclaimed and influential works including *A Realist Theory of Science*, *The Possibility of Naturalism*, *Scientific Realism and Human Emancipation*, *Reclaiming Reality* and *Dialectic: The Pulse of Freedom*. He is an editor of the recently published *Critical Realism: Essential Readings* and is currently chair of the Centre for Critical Realism.

CRITICAL REALISM: INTERVENTIONS SERIES
Edited by Margaret Archer, Roy Bhaskar, Andrew Collier, Tony Lawson and Alan Norrie

CRITICAL REALISM
Essential Readings
Edited by Margaret Archer, Roy Bhaskar, Andrew Collier, Tony Lawson and Alan Norrie

BEING AND WORTH
Andrew Collier

THE POSSIBILITY OF NATURALISM
A Philosophical Critique of the Contemporary Human Sciences
Roy Bhaskar

QUANTUM THEORY AND THE FLIGHT FROM REALISM
Philosophical Responses to Quantum Mechanics
Chris Norris

FROM EAST TO WEST
Odyssey of a Soul
Roy Bhaskar

FROM EAST TO WEST

Odyssey of a Soul

Roy Bhaskar

London and New York

First published 2000
by Routledge
11 New Fetter Lane, London EC4P 4EE

Simultaneously published in the USA and Canada
by Routledge
29 West 35th Street, New York, NY 10001

Routledge is an imprint of the Taylor & Francis Group

Typeset in Perpetua by Taylor & Francis Books Ltd
Printed and bound in Great Britain by Clays Ltd, St Ives plc

British Library Cataloguing in Publication Data
A catalogue record for this book is available from the British Library

Library of Congress Cataloging in Publication Data
Bhaskar, Roy, 1944–
From east to west: odyssey of a soul/Roy Bhaskar.
(Critical realism–interventions)
Includes bibliographical references and index.
1. Religion–Philosophy. 2. Critical realism. 3. Philosophy, Comparative. 4. Self-realization. I. Series.

BL51.B554 2000 99-087584
181'.4–dc21

ISBN 0–415–23324–0 (hbk)
ISBN 0–415–23325–9 (pbk)

TO MIKE ROBINSON

CONTENTS

PREFACE AND ACKNOWLEDGEMENTS

The essential thesis of this book is that man is essentially God (and therefore also essentially one, but also essentially unique); and that, as such, he is essentially free and already en-lightened, a freedom and enlightenment which is overlain by extraneous, heteronomous determinations which both (a) occlude and (b) qualify this essential fact. To reclaim and realise his essential freedom, man has to shed both the illusion that he is not essentially Godlike and free and the constraining heteronomous determinations (constituting an objective world of illusion, duality and alienation) which that illusion grounds. To become free or realise his freedom man must thus shed both the illusions that he is not (essentially) and that he is (already, only and completely) free! Surprisingly enough this is a position anticipated in the traditions of both radical libertarian Western thought and mystical Eastern thought, between which *From East to West* aspires to begin to construct a dialogue, bridge and synthesis. Since God is also – or so I argue – *inter alia* unconditional love (unbounded peace and infinite joy or happiness) and we are essentially Godlike, the most appropriate (correct, best possible) ethical and political stance is one of unconditional love for our essential selves, and that of each and every other being and the environment we inhabit. This in turn entails non-judgemental observation combined with engaged (but unattached) activity in the world. In these and other respects, the book is also an attempted reconciliation of some of the best insights of the New Age and the New Left movements. As should be obvious from what I have already said, and as I outline in the introduction to the book and systematise in the general theoretical introduction in Part I, *From East to West* also constitutes a very radical development of the existing philosophy of (dialectical) critical realism into a philosophy of and for universal self-realisation. On this philosophy the basic structure of both man and the world (of which man forms a part) is God; and man's essential task is to realise this transcendental or categorial fact. Nothing in this book involves the rejection of any existing (dialectical) critical realist position. Rather it constitutes a development, albeit only one possible development, of dialectical critical realism, involving a further transcendental radicalisation of it, entailing *inter alia* a new realism about transcendence and God; the nature and persistence of the self; life as a dialectical learning process; and the unmediated, spontaneous and natural (at once free and lawful) character of best possible action, grounding objective morality in the intrinsic nature of the self (including the uniquely individuated, concretely singularised, universality of our Godlike essence).

The book consists of essentially two parts: a theoretical part, in which I show how dialectical critical realism must develop into a philosophy of (universal) self-realisation, which can be characterised as a transcendental dialectical critical realism; and a narrative novella, in which I further develop and exemplify this philosophy, in particular so as to attempt to substantiate the ideas of reincarnation, *karma* and *moksha* or liberation. For the philosophy I am indebted to generations – one could say millennia – of teachers, some of whom are encountered in the narrative. For the details of the narrative, which makes no claim to (though it might be or contain) historical truth, and much else besides I am indebted to Mike Robinson, to whom the book is dedicated, and also to Kenny Pask. To both of them my warmest heartfelt thanks for their time and friendship; and also to Stephanie Spindler for the cover of the book, which inspired me during the final stages of its writing. At a personal level, I must first and foremost record a deep debt of gratitude to Bridget Oakley. But I am also warmly appreciative of the help of many, countless friends. Amongst them, however, I must mention and thank Maggie Erotokritou, Martha Sylvester, Maggie Levine, Alistair Shearer, Felicity Kaplan and Romy Jacob. In a very special category, I must also warmly thank for their friendship and support my friends and colleagues in the Centre for Critical Realism and International Association of Critical Realism, including especially Maggie Archer, Andrew Collier, Tony Lawson, Alan Norrie, Sean Vertigan, Mervyn Hartwig and Doug Porpora. I am also extremely indebted to my publisher, Alan Jarvis, for the prompt publication of this book and for his general encouragement and support both for it and for the *Critical Realism: Interventions* Series. I am also extremely grateful to Ted Benton, William Outhwaite, the much lamented late Roy Edgley, Terry Eagleton, Rom Harré, Kate Soper, Peter Manicas, Sue Clegg, Chris Norris, Michael Sprinker, Andrew Sayer, Gary MacLennan, Colin Robinson, Stephan Chambers, Sebastian Budgen and Hilary Wainwright (amongst innumerable others) for their help and friendship over the years. I would like to reiterate my gratitude for and appreciation of all the help and support I have had from so many others who I have not been able to mention specifically in the Preface. This, however, I cannot conclude without recording my appreciation of and thanks to Gweneth Kell and Jenny Cobner for typing the manuscript.

Roy Bhaskar
Brahmes Hall, Suffolk
10 November 1999

INTRODUCTION TO THE BOOK

This book describes the odyssey of a soul on its journey to enlightenment. It is essentially about transcending alienation or split, both inner and outer, through a dialectical learning process in which division, ignorance and illusion (and the attachments and aversions, cravings and conditionalities, suffering and oppression they ground, induce and cause) are progressively overcome in the course of a sequence of lives which the soul experiences and the book describes. Fifteen lives, listed in chronological order below, are dealt with in some detail, and a few others are discussed more abruptly. Of course the soul has had many more lives, and many more even within the time span considered. The lives described are those which appear most immediately relevant to the fulfilment of the soul's intention: to bring perennial truth into the compass of an adventure story. Several great world belief systems – including Ancient Greek, Judaic, Essene and Christian, (Vedic) Hindu, Buddhist, Confucian, Taoist, Zen, (Sufi) Islam and modern materialist thought – are encountered; and partly to accommodate this, *From East To West* is articulated into nine chapters, each treating one or more life. This narrative of the dialectical progression of lives is itself preceded by a general theoretical introduction, which in a sense belongs to life fifteen, insofar as it considers some pertinent aspects of the development of the philosophy of critical realism towards a philosophy of and for (ultimately, and necessarily, universal) self-realisation. Each system or world view in turn points to and contributes to the fulfilment of the soul's ultimate vocation as an enlightened spiritual teacher.

In this introduction, I want to do two things. The first aim is to preface the general theoretical introduction and so begin to contextualise *From East To West* in contemporary philosophy. The second is to outline, at similar length, a brief abstract or synopsis of the lives described in the book. In order to accomplish the first, I briefly sketch the content of the four sections of the introduction, which correspond roughly to the four moments of dialectical critical realism; and then, after briefly recapitulating the development of critical realism into the system of dialectical critical realism I elaborated in *Dialectic: The Pulse of Freedom* (London:

Verso, 1993, hereafter referred to as *DPF* (and recapitulated in *Plato Etc.* (London: Verso, 1994, hereafter referred to as *PE*)), I use it to cast light on contemporary crises in Western (and tendentially, asymptotically, global) social and philosophical (including scientific) thought. These themselves reflect wider and deeper crises in society, which I will relate to a dialectical chain of *avidya* (ignorance, understood here especially, but not exclusively, as categorial error), *dualism* (or split) and *maya* (or illusion), itself grounded in ontological (existential) *insecurity*, manifested as fear or desire (which may be seen as (real) perspectival switches on each other), and the *alienation* of (embodied) human beings from their true selves and the rest of the cosmos.

The abstract of lives in this foreword is fairly self-explanatory, but in the narrative of the book I exemplify and develop the philosophy of universal self-realisation sketched in the introduction. I am well aware that in *From East To West* I am appealing to two different (although partially overlapping) constituencies of readers, between which, indeed, the book aspires to contribute to the construction of some kind of bridge. At any rate,. I hope that those without a formal philosophical background will glean something from the more philosophical aspects of the narrative, though they may want to skip (at least on a first read), or at best merely skim, the general theoretical introduction in Part I and possibly Part A of this introduction to the book.

A Preview of theory

From East To West will be followed by works of theoretical philosophy in the idiom of *A Realist Theory of Science* (London: Verso, 1997, hereafter referred to as *RTS*), *The Possibility of Naturalism* (3rd edition, London: Routledge, 1998, hereafter referred to as *PON*) and *Dialectic: The Pulse of Freedom* (*DPF*). The point of the introduction is to indicate something of its relationship to, and in particular the sense in which it both presupposes and establishes a progressive development of, the content of the existing philosophy of critical realism. The introduction is divided into four sections, which systematically work through respectively the four moments or levels of dialectical critical realism: 1M, of ontology; 2E, of absence (dialectic and negativity); 3L, of totality (internal relationality and holistic causality) and 4D, of agency or transformative praxis, i.e. creative work (and absolute reason or the unity of theory in practice in practice, ultimately and only in 'cosmic consciousness' or enlightenment).

The first section, dealing with 1M, is itself delineated into four sub-sections. In the first I discuss the much maligned and misunderstood, but indispensable and inexorable, topic of *ontology*. I then specifically highlight the ways in which transcendental realism is committed to both a *dispositional* and a *categorial realism* (in the second and third sub-sections respectively). In the final sub-section I then move on to thematise the existence of *God*, as an absolute but actualised ground of pure dispositionality which is also the ultimate categorial structure of the world, including man, so that God is at once both (at least in part) ontologically immanent and epistemically (and (mainly) experientially) transcendent.

The second section, treating 2E, pivots on the core notion of *absence*, with its characteristic negative and positive *duality*. Here I look once more at Hegelian dialectic. Its rational kernel is an epistemological learning, more generally *developmental*, *process*. This process metatheoretically informs the infrastructure of the narrative of the book, and in particular underpins the interconnected triad of ideas of *reincarnation*, *karma* – or 'quantum (or holistic) natural law' – and *moksha*, or liberation – ideas which can be deduced from the emergent powers – where emergence is a positive bi-polar dual or outcome of absence – of intentional states. The motor of the learning process, the dialectic that drives the dialectic of and in *From East To West*, turns formally on *incompleteness* or lack, and substantially on *desire* or *fear* (or other emotional states derivative from attachment or (ultimately) self-alienation). Reverting to the Hegelian dialectic, its mystical shell is *ontological monovalence* or the absence of (the concept and, in crucial respects, the reality or presence of) absence. Within its mystical shell is a golden nugget, the dialectics of co-presence, including the *co-presence* of levels of absolute or independent, relative or dependent and false (or demi-real, illusory) dependent being. Finally, the mystical shell reveals a fourth element or platinum plate, highlighting its *diagnostic value* as the absence of absence undergirds the demi-real or 'myopic' categorial structure of contemporary society or four-planar social being.

The dialectic critique of purely analytical reason (and the notions of identity, subjectivity and objectivity which the latter implies) leads into the third section, exploring the 3L role of totality.[1] This includes such topics as identity, internal relationality, subjectivity and objectivity, universality and singularity, abstraction and concretion, things and events, and holistic, heterocosmic (including amplified and reversed), reflexive and quantum causality. A radical account of the *self* emerges. What is normally understood by the self is an (illicit) abstraction from a much deeper and broader totality. The stratified, rhythmically developing, concretely singularised – and vastly expanded – concept of the self leads naturally on to the terrain of the fourth section, treating the 4D domain of transformative praxis. This section may be contextualised by reflecting on the immortal dialogue between Krishna and Arjuna in the *Bhagavad Gita* as the opposing armies of the Pandavas and Kauravas prepare to face and fight each other on the (Armageddonesque) field of Kurukshetra. Arjuna's question, 'what am I to do?',

1 *From East To West* is the first of a series of books which will foreground 3L and subsequently 4D. In *Dialectic: The Pulse of Freedom*, the primary emphasis was on 2E.

and Krishna's response, which is in effect an answer to the question, 'who am I?', reflect pressing current questions of *agency* and *identity* (at 4D and 3L respectively in the architectonic of dialectical critical realism (DCR)). To act in accordance with our Godlike but concretely singularised (specific and uniquely individuated) *dharma* or real nature (or essence) is to act *spontaneously correctly*, with *least effort* and *maximum coherence*. To act in this manner we (only!) have to realise or become who or what we essentially are. And for this realisation or becoming, Krishna prescribes a *dialectic* or *dialectics* of *inaction* and *action*.

On the terrain of 4D, briefly in the general theoretical introduction (for they will be exemplified in detail in the course of the narrative), I then go on to describe the mechanism of spontaneous right (or optimum, best) action, the dynamics of liberation or enlightenment, the criterion of absolute reason or the unity of theory in practice in practice, and the nature of the 'social cube' situated in (here generalised) 'four-planar social space'. Once again, a radical account of our agentive agency (our embodied creative praxis) is forthcoming. Moreover the dialectic of the desire to freedom, that is also from desire (or fear) to freedom, understood as Self-determination and connoting at once (individual) autonomy and universal flourishing or eudaimonia – i.e. the free development of each as a condition of the free development of all – which underpins the pulse to freedom (in *DPF*) now manifests itself as a *dialectic* (or dialectics) of *self-realisation*. This involves *inter alia* action without attachment (or aversion). Ultimately the dialectic of self-realisation ushers in a dialectic of *God-realisation*, conveying (in one sense or inflection of 'God-realisation') the conatus to the embodiment of heaven on earth. In such a state, concretely singularised Self-centred subjects flourish in selfless solidarity with each and all in 'unity existence' (*being and doing*). This is not a mere pipe dream, or so I argue, but a presupposition of our most elemental desire or our first, most primordial, fear.

In a theoretical sequel to this book, I will formally relate (in a way which is only hinted at here) Marx's critique of political economy as a causally aefficacious[2] ideology to a Vedantian critique of the dualistic and fragmented, alienated (myopic, egocentric) world of *maya* or illusion which most of us inhabit solely, or so it seems. In this sequel, probably to be entitled *Transcendence and Totality*, I will thematise the present book, in the context of East–West relations generally, under the somewhat polemical and deliberately provocative rubric of the 'Rise and Fall of the West'. Western culture is now an increasingly global culture, and we are arguably on the threshold of its demise. Dominant Western accounts of society and knowledge and more especially the demi-real (false, illusory but casually aefficacious and so (though dependently and relatively) real) categorial

2 So spelt as to bring out its *a*ffective as well as its *e*ffective power.

structures which inform them threaten the survival of our and other species on the planet, and even the planet itself. *Demystification* can ultimately only be *liberation*. To and in such an enlightened society, partially though dimly prefigured as the new millennium dawns, both West and East (and North and South), in the odyssey of the soul this book describes, have something to offer and nothing to lose. To *reclaim* and *re-enchant reality* we have only to become what we really, essentially, truly, are and will never cease to be, however occluded that realisation currently appears.

Critical realism, the web of illusion and contemporary thought

I now want to discuss briefly the development of critical realism into the system of dialectical critical realism and to show how each of the moments or levels of DCR, as just outlined, can be related to persistent problems of (as well as, dialectically, some recent progressive features in) contemporary social thought; and more briefly (for this will be treated at length in the main body of the theoretical introduction and in the narrative of the book) how these aporiai offer diagnostic clues or appear as symptoms of ills in the nature of contemporary social reality or human being itself. Metacritically, this is characterised by a *dialectical chain*, constituted by *absence* (in its normatively negative mode), betokening *incompleteness* of a radical sort, leading to *error* (specifically categorial error) or *avidya* (ignorance) and *illusion* (maya), generating *contradictions* (inconsistencies) and *split* (division), producing *dualism* and fragmentation, split-off and *alienation*. This results in its wake, when what is split off (alienated), supressed or excluded is nevertheless categorially or axiologically necessary, in *denegation*, namely the expression or affirmation of what is denied (despite or even in its denial) in what I have called a *tina compromise form* (see *DPF* C 2.7),[3] and thence to *reflexive inconsistency* and *performative contradiction*. This chain of *avidya* secretes a veil[4] or veils, which together form an interlocking *web* or meshwork of *illusions*. This (irrealist) web (or ensemble) holds contemporary thought in thrall, generating aporiai,

3 This is the general categorial form of a society or being characterised by the co-existence (co-presence) of *necessary* and emergent *unnecessary*, constraining (occluding, oppressive or otherwise injurious) supplementary *determinations*, whether ingrained, dispositionally, as habits, attachments, *karma*, the presence of the past, blocks and so on, and whether manifest in cognitive (for example, as illusion) or non-cognitive (for example, as a constraining impurity or additional draining determination) modes or both. Liberation consists in the *disemergence* of these supplementary determinations, these extraneous constraints on the realisation of the true categorial nature of man.

4 Note a veil not only hides or *obscures* but dialectically both (covers and) *protects* (and therefore keeps pure, intact and whole) and stands at the *threshold* to the reality, whether absolute or relative, it occludes. It thus constitutes a starting point for dialectical penetration or development, a premise for *immanent critique* and a phenomenon for *retroductive explanation*.

contradictions, lacunae, conflicts, splits, anomalies, crises and many other modes of oppositionality (see *PE*, pp. 242–3) within it.

These alienations, contradictions and so on within thought and between thought and the reality it is about are to be explained in terms of the real alienations and contradictions at all four planes of social being, i.e. within socialised reality itself, and specifically in terms of its irreal but causally aefficacious demi-real categorial structure[5] grounded in ontological monovalence (both conceptual and real). This *real alienation* (and the *conceptual alienation* to which it gives rise) is in turn ultimately to be explained in terms of *self-alienation*, both inner and outer,[6] that is the alienation of embodied human beings from their true natures and the social totality (and ultimately cosmos) they inhabit; and the insecurity, fear, attachment, instrumental reasoning, conditionality, reification, suffering and oppression which it engenders.

This self-alienation or dis-unity (or self-division) can only be remedied by a practice or *yoga* (union) of de-alienation or re-union in a dialectic in which the typical (absolute, other-worldly, transcendental) emphases of the East on the enduring deep stratification of human being, on accessing a higher superconscious self, on non-attachment, being and individual liberation (on absence and inaction) are complemented by the characteristic (relative, this-worldly, immanent) emphases of the West on the other planes of social being, on disengaging unconscious mechanisms, on material embodiment, engaged activity and collective emancipation (on presence and action). This dialectic or yoga of de-alienation, of self-consciousness in engaged but unattached activity, propelled by (unconditional) love, is ultimately a dialectic not only of Self-realisation but (in one sense of that term) of God-realisation, where God is understood *inter alia* as the abiding and ultimate real categorial structure of the world which the web of *maya*, secreting multiple levels of alienation (*tina* compromise formation and (extraneous)

5 This categorial structure is:
(1) *Irrealist* in character (i.e. not realist);
(2) *Demi-real* in truth-value (i.e. false) but
(3) *Real* in causal aefficacy (and hence being), although dependently so.

6 That is to say, this *intrinsic* self-alienation is not only *internal* but also *external* (see *RTS*, pp. 76–7), so that what is intrinsic to the self also includes beings who lie outside its spatial (or auric) envelope, as well as relations (and attitudes to relations) with such entities or beings. Accordingly, self-alienation has two aspects, sources or manifestations: inner self-alienation is characteristically from depth, and outer self-alienation characteristically from totality. But not all outer alienation and division is necessarily or immediately self-alienation, although it may relationally cause or induce it. It is only, as we shall see (in Part 1), at (or from) a certain refined level of consciousness or perception that the old Vedic formula 'I am totality' holds; and its development presupposes the (and does not abolish the sense in which there remains) *prior* differentiation of selves from others. Moreover, unity is not the same as, though it includes, identity. Nor is a being's identity fixed, rather it is a process in development. Similarly not all alienation (for example, alienation of contingent or non-essential properties) is self-alienation.

heteronomous constraining determination), obscures (screens, veils), dislocates and distorts.

As hitherto developed, critical realism has four main moments or benchmarks: transcendental realism; critical naturalism; the theory of explanatory critique; and dialectic as dialectically developed and systematically presented in dialectical critical realism. Each moment presupposes the earlier one(s) and each may be represented by a relatively canonical book (*RTS*, *PON*, *Scientific Realism and Human Emancipation* (London: Verso, 1986, hereafter referred to as *SRHE*) and *DPF* respectively). They may be regarded as showing respectively how science, social science, objective morality and absence and (thence) emancipation, and also causality, process and change (and hence the possibilities not only of doubt, desire and fear but also of creativity, love and freedom) was both possible and necessary, in opposition to dominant orthodoxies and fashionable heterodoxies which, in one way or another, scouted or could not sustain them.

Transcendental realism was oriented against the epistemic fallacy, the definition or analysis of being in terms of human knowing, and the actualism (the reduction of powers to their exercise, the possible to the actual, the self to agency or behaviour, being to doing) and closure of existing accounts of science. It argued for the stratification, differentiation and openness of the world (and, as one part of it, human scientific knowledge). Critical naturalism inveighs against the splits, dualisms and dichotomies (the terms of which are characteristically, but shiftingly, asymmetrically charged or aefficacious) that plagued the then (*c.*1979) contemporary human sciences – and to a large extent continue to do so. These splits include those between positivistic naturalism and hermeneutical anti-naturalism, individualism and collectivism, structure and agency, reason and cause, mind and body and fact and value. In each case a third transcending or sublating position, such as critical naturalism, relationism, the transformational model of social activity, synchronic emergent powers materialism and so on, was motivated. The theory of explanatory critique was directed against one of these dichotomies in particular, namely the fact/value one, and especially Hume's law that one cannot derive an 'ought' from an 'is'. Its epistemic status is on a par with that of social science, insofar as to disallow the inference from fact to value because it is subject (in inevitably, and inexorably, open systems) to a *ceteris paribus* clause (or clauses) logically compels rejection of the inference from fact to fact on the same ground (see *Critical Realism: Essential Readings* (*CR:ER*), p. xix, and also *SRHE* C2.5–7).

The central thrust of the dialectic, in dialectical critical realism, was against ontological monovalence, namely the generation of a purely positive account of being, the absenting of the concept of absence, which it identified as the cardinal error of Western philosophy from Parmenides to the present day, and so in a sense underpinned the other errors fastened upon by the earlier moments of critical realism. The present book in a way initiates a *fifth* development by seeing, as already indicated, the alienation of embodied human beings – physically embedded in 'four-planar social being' (see *DPF* C2.9 and passim) – from their true natures and the rest of the cosmos as underwriting and expressed by ontological monovalence and (hence) the other categorial errors. It may be viewed either as a development *within* DCR accentuating 3L (and 4D), or a development *beyond* it (which however presupposes it) to a transcendental or *T*DCR.

Each of the four existing stadia of DCR: 1M, of ontology and realism; 2E, of absence, dialectic and negativity; 3L, of totality, internal relationality and holistic causality; and 4D, of transformative praxis (agentive agency and creative work) and absolute reason (or the unity of theory and practice in practice)

(a) may be related, as a response, to a characteristic form of scepticism;
(b) may be iteratively applied to, or recursively embedded within, each other;
(c) positively, may be associated with a recent (or not so recent) progressive turn in social thought;
(d) negatively, may be used to cast light on a nexus of contemporary aporiai or crises in social thought and life generally;
(e) in particular, in virtue of the diagnostic value of philosophy, revealing the split-and-combined *tina* compromise-formed character of contemporaneously actually existing social life and human being, especially in the *dialectic* of (the co-presence of necessary (autonomous) and emergent but unnecessary) *heteronomous determinations*, the resolution of which in (ultimately universal) Self-realisation is a main theme of the book, and so will not be discussed any further here in this introduction.

Thus to exemplify (a) we have:

at 1M, scepticism about *being* generally, including the very reality of an external world, of causality, the existence of other persons (not to mention lives) and of God, the transcendent and transcendence generally;

at 2E, scepticism about *process* (that is, about being-in-motion) and progress including justice (the spectre raised by the problem of relativism) and the questions posed by the possibilities of reincarnation and *karma* (and freedom from both);

at 3L, scepticism (or at least concern) about *identity*, including the nature of the self (the existential predicament – 'who am I?' – or, in its communitarian guise, 'who are we?') and about totality, wholeness and holistic causality, and

at 4D, scepticism (or angst) about (agentive) *agency* (the axiological dilemma: 'what am I (are we) to do?' (or the Leninist 'what is to be done?')) and about consciousness, self-consciousness, freedom as autonomy or self-determination (liberation, enlightenment and self-realisation).

Immediately following on from this, and in illustration of (b), we have realism about ontology, science and truth at 1D, about absence, process and change at 2E, about internal relations, totality and the self at 3L, and about agency, consciousness, reflexivity (self-consciousness) and freedom as autonomy or self-determination at 4D.

In respect of (c), 1M may be related to a recent *realist* (ontological) turn in social (including scientific) thought, and 3L to growing *ecological* or environmental – and more generally holistic – concerns, a green turn, which I elaborate on in Part I. Developments at 2E can be mapped on to a processual or a red turn and at 4D to a reflexive one. If the processual term has nineteenth-century roots, the reflexive one has even earlier ones. Initiated – at least in modernity – or more properly re-initiated by Descartes, and then progressively radicalised in association with the theme of self-consciousness by Kant, Hegel and Marx and the other so-called 'masters' of (the hermeneutics of) suspicion, Nietzche and Freud, it has characteristically taken the form, in the twentieth century, of a preoccupation with language as the means and medium (and even totality) of our understandings, social interaction and access to reality, veering so far as the denial of the intelligible reference to anything other than or outside language, for example in the shape of the 'linguistic fallacy', *viz.* the reduction or analysis of being to or in terms of our language about being (including language). In its broadest compass, however, reflexivity may be turned into a powerful criterion for the acceptability or otherwise of any philosophy. A philosophy is acceptable only if it can adequately sustain and situate itself; and in particular, its content, context and production. Only DCR, and more especially the TDCR outlined in this book, can satisfy this criterion; or, so I argue. Moreover any philosophy satisfying such a criterion will, I shall contend, carry a conatus to the goal of universal self-realisation, that is for the whole of the totality of all beings, in what I have called 'unity existence'.

Other philosophies are theory/practice inconsistent, i.e. commit performative contradiction. Indeed irrealism constitutes an *antinomic–dilemmatic* interlocking package or *ensemble*, from which, once entered, there is scant chance of escape. Thus irrealism about tense leads to irrealism about causality and thence to irrealism about existence, the self and the subject, the (or one) starting point of the irrealist exercise, which in this way collapses in on itself. Irrealism is thus an auto-subversive internally contradictory ensemble, in which mutually inconsistent positions are held in place in compromise formations (invoked when required) by the web of *lived illusion* – this is *maya* as *practical ideology* – that is the chain of *avidya*, and which constitutes the demi-real categorial structure of societies characterised by the alienation of human beings from their true natures and the rest of the cosmos, producing inner and outer conflict and split, and the ontological monovalence which at once expresses and sustains this and at the same time makes it unthinkable (and with it the very thought of thought itself). In contrast, realism, and in particular (transcendental) dialectical critical realism, goes some way to satisfying the bar of absolute reason, the unity of theory and practice in practice (at least in theoretical practice). Moreover its goal, the conatus it carries is nothing other or less than universal self-realisation, enlightenment or freedom, universal or absolute eudaimonia.

Turning now to (d), contemporary social thought is characterised by destratification and closure at 1M, deprocessualisation and endism at 2E,[7] detotalisation and alienation at 3L and deagentification and reification at 4D. These features are associated with aporiai and oppositions around, as already noted under (a), *being* at 1M, *change* (including progress and development, turning on absence and its paradigmatically positive dual or correlative, emergence) at 2E, *identity* (including individuation and selfhood) at 3L and *agency* and *freedom* (including consciousness and creativity, reflexivity and self-consciousness) at 4D.

Underlying these properties are a fourfold denegation: at 1M, of *ontology*; at 2E, of *absence*; at 3L, of *totality*; and at 4D, of *agentive agency*.[8] The denegation of ontology at 1M is reflected in scepticism (or agnosticism) about science, truth (including alethic truth), transcendence and God (see (a) above). The denegation of absence (and emergence, i.e. its potential emergent product) at 2E is manifest in a whole series of characteristically asymmetrically weighted or charged dualisms or splits, such as those besetting the human sciences already noticed; and more generally those stemming from the (unstateable, on ontological monovalence) primal generative separation or alienation of man from God (which encompasses his alienation from both his true self and the totality it inhabits). This generative separation both underpins and is reinforced by the radical incompleteness of the chain of *avidya* and the web of *maya* which veils the absent self or totality. Second, the denegation of absence is reflected in problems of relativism,

7 This reached its apogee in the triumphalist rhetoric of the 'end of history' associated with the collapse around 1989 of 'actually existing socialism' as manifest in the communist states. The most influential exposition of this was Fukuyama's *The End of History and the Last Man* (London, 1992), for a critique of which see *DPF*, p. 376n.

8 As already pointed out, denegation takes the form of *explicit* denial combined with, and – insofar as what is explicitly denied is categorially and so (also) axiologically necessary – necessarily combined with, *implicit* or tacit presupposition (and therefore affirmation), in the content or context of what is said or done (for example, in a tina compromise form), of some species of what is denied. Thus empiricism secretes an implicit ontology and an implicit realism – of empirical realism. This must perforce also summon up and utilise critical, and even dialectical critical, realist features to sustain itself in a (dialectically) critically realist world environment. In this fashion, as already indicated, it is auto-subversive (self-deconstructive) or reflexively inconsistent: the force of the dialectical critique.

manifest, for example, in scepticism about the possibility of progress or justice (see (b) above).

The denegation of totality at 3L has a number of effects. First, it results in a whole series of alienations at the different overlapping levels (conceptual, real, self) already noted. Second, it encourages a tendency towards analytic extentionalism or romantic expressionism, the non-dialectical or undifferentiated restriction of reason to purely analytical or else expressivist modes of thought. Third, it inculcates scepticism about totalities and identities, including the constitution of subjects and subjectivity, normally (mis)understood in an unstratified, fixed (undeveloping) and unmediated, often atomistic and punctualist manner; and that of objects and objectivity, characteristically (mis)taken in abstract, undialectical and reified or otherwise atomistic terms, together with that of their relations.[9]

The denegation of agentive agency at 4D leads to reflexive inconsistency – for instance, in split-and-combined philosophical formations – as for example in the antinomic combination of mutually exclusive forms of free will and determinism.[10] More particularly, it results in a tendency to the hypostasis, alienation or extrusion of philosophy, or the discursive act in which it or some particular philosophical position is expressed from the totality or field it is about or in which it is expressed. It is also marked in scepticism about the possibility of an objective morality or *dharma* (which will be both subject-specific and concretely singularised). And a scepticism, as has already been noted, about consciousness, self-consciousness and freedom; and (to bring 1M–4D together) in scepticism about the possibility of an underlying or enduring self (or soul) which persists (although perhaps only dispositionally) through disembodiment and changes of embodiment and develops, progressing in a dialectical learning process (governed by quantum natural law) towards self-consciousness or self-realisation which is also self-determination or freedom.

In the general theoretical introduction in Part I, which I have here been previewing and prefacing, I work systematically through the moments of DCR, as developed in TDCR. My aim there is, in part, to show how the denegations, dualisms, alienations and reflexive inconsistencies (1M–4D) of contemporary thought can be resolved in a dialectic of self-realisation which is at once self-transcendence in a deeper (the Eastern emphasis) and wider (the Western one)

9 Thus we have the notion of things as fixed and events as punctiform; universality as abstract (rather than concrete) and objectivity as unrelativised.

10 Or in Rorty's attempt in his influential *Philosophy and the Mirror of Nature* (Oxford, 1979) to advance both eliminative materialism in Part I (which must eliminate the intelligibility of philosophical discourse) and, in Part III, conversational hermeneutics which is excluded by it (but is a necessary (quasi-Derridean) 'supplement' for its very 'effability' (expression or thought – producing a typical tina compromise formation). For a critique, see my *Philosophy and the Idea of Freedom* (Oxford: Blackwell, 1991), especially C2.

totality and the unravelling of the layers of the web of illusion, packed like onion peel, which occlude the existence of God as the ultimate categorial structure of the world including our socialised being.

I now move on to the abstract of lives, which I begin by listing in chronological order.

B Abstract of lives

Lives in approximate chronological order

Life One	Crossing the Red Sea with Moses: the teacher [red] (a sort of idyllic, and the holy grail).
Life Two	In Ancient Greece (I): the philosopher [orange] – from Pythagoras to Laozi (to Plato) and the illusions of *soma*.
Life Three	In Ancient Greece (II): the orchard [yellow] – or Orpheus in the underworld and the perils of attachment.
Life Four	Scrolling: the writer [green] – (in Qumran: joy, unconditionality and service).
Life Five	From Galilee to Kashmir: meeting the Master [blue] (transcending fear and the expanded self).
Life Six	The itinerant Cardinal (northern–central Italy) – the mediator and explorer [purple] – voyages of discovery (and from West to East (III)).
Life Seven	The warlord (Japan) [red]: the Rising Sun and the divided mind.
Life Eight	In China (I): the emergent heart and a life in bondage [yellow].
Life Nine	In China (II): A Taoist dawn and the middle truth: in search of balance, the quest for nothing (emptiness) and enlightenment in alienation [blue].
Life Ten	In Tibet: a Himalayan heartbeat [indigo] – or compassion and the void (from individual liberation to universal self-realisation).
Life Eleven	In India: the guru [violet]: transcendence and totality – or from the path of renunciation to the path of action.
Life Twelve	In the Near East: the (Sufi) Sultan [red] – or from the way of the recluse to the way of the householder (or experiencing the extremities of the socio-economic world (I)).
Life Thirteen	Poverty in southern Italy (Amalfi): the outcast [yellow] – experiencing the extremities of the socio-economic world (II).
Life Fourteen	The French philosopher: the (sceptical) mystic [silver/indigo] – mapping the contours of (socialised) human being.

Life Fifteen The circle completed: from East to West: liberation (and the path to enlightenment) [gold/white/violet].

For the purposes of this abstract, I will describe the lives that constitute the karmic chain and *dharma* of the soul in chronological order.

[The Arian Age]

A young child crosses the Red Sea, in the company of his parents and siblings, with Moses at the age of seven. He lives to be a great age, is happily married and has three children (two boys and a girl). He learns his father's trade as a potter but his vocation is to be a teacher, in which he is schooled by Moses and his immediate circle. He teaches the children of the chosen people, in small groups of three or four, the esoteric teachings of the perennial wisdom. In life five he will follow the apple of his eye, his eldest son, and start his mandate of teaching the unconverted. In this life we see our hero as a youth and an adult successfully negotiating his way through the perils of the various initiations necessary to assume the vocation of spiritual teacher. Though a life of trial, tribulation and hardship, this is nevertheless a happy life, in which the soul begins to acquire an understanding of the principles and purposes of his destiny. It is naturally connected with lives four and five and indeed other Judaic and Christian lives, especially life six.

In life two the soul appears in Ancient Greece, again as a teacher (to the sons of the rich). Under the influence of Pythagoras, an enormous, expansive mind roams the stars at night and ponders their meaning by day. He travels east to Babylon, Persia and India (spending five or six years in or around northern India); west to Italy; south to Egypt (where he comes across remnants of the buried Atlantian civilisation) and north to the various Greek settlements. Languages come to him easily. He teaches dialectic and investigates the mysteries of being. In Chapter 2 he is interrogated by his counterpart in life fourteen, who shares many of his interests and some of his fame. He predicts eclipses and earthquakes, he argues and heals, uses symbols and signs and he is never still: a bumble bee. He sees himself as completing the work of Pythagoras by bringing the wisdom of the East (including some sacred Vedic texts and Buddha's oral teaching) to the West.

In life three the soul is again reincarnated in Ancient Greece, but this time as a woman. Coming from a powerful and learned family, she is betrothed at an early age into a family of similar caste. But the menfolk are away at war and she takes on responsibility for educating the young (although she is to remain childless herself). She shares the interests of her predecessor in life two and becomes a member of a secret cult, whose symbol is the apple. Half-muse, half-oracle, she practises an extreme form of Pythagorean vegetarianism, eating only fruit, especially lemons and oranges; and eventually dies at an early age from malnutrition. She is however a strong woman, and has dreamed of a former age – in Atlantian times – when women and especially priestesses were dominant. This sets up a yearning for balance between male and female aspects which can only be achieved in a coming age of enlightenment.

In life four we see him as a scribe in the Essene headquarters at Qumran by the Dead Sea, busily at work with some others on the texts which have become known as the Dead Sea Scrolls. He is at one with the angelic forces of night and day, and he shares the lifestyles and beliefs of his Essene brothers and sisters. This is a happy and long life, spent in harmony with nature and his fellow human beings. If life one establishes his vocation as a teacher and life two as a philosopher, the soul has by now, in this and the preceding lives, established his vocation as a writer.

[The Piscean Age]

In life five he is born in Galilee and catches a glimpse of Jesus as a youth. He studies and practises his teachings. He becomes a teacher himself, but is full of fear. Jesus appears to him twenty years after the crucifixion in a dream and summons him to Kashmir, where he is currently teaching. Our hero mounts a momentous journey to meet the master in which he is robbed, assaulted and abused, until finally clad only in loin cloth and armed with his trusty pen, hungry and parched, he arrives at his destination. He meets Jesus after a night's sleep. They walk and talk in a garden by the temple in which he is staying in the following day for several hours. The soul loses its fear and his heart is opened. He commits himself with renewed vigour for his task and returns to Palestine, but his teachings are ignored and he dies about the time of the Roman assault on Massada.

In the next life – nearly one thousand four hundred years later – to be considered, the soul is reborn in northern Italy to a great and noble family. Of spiritual disposition and with a mind of tremendous fluency he sets out to resolve the disputes raging across the Renaissance, so-called 'enlightened' world. He uses his influence and teaches his students to mediate the truths of science and religion. Indeed, he is a negotiator–mediator par excellence. Wherever there is a dispute he will set out to, and usually succeed, in settling it.

In the first thirty years or so of this life he is primarily the intellectual, but his temperament is spiritual and he takes his vows and quite soon becomes a cardinal. At the age of forty-five he travels to Portugal and begins a momentous voyage, at the Pope's request (with conversion and trade equally in mind), along the coast of Africa to the East. He is fascinated by India, stopping for some time in Goa and Calcutta, and also China and the closed territory of Japan. This follows the pattern of lives two and five, going east to bring wisdom back to the west, and it is this same theme which sets up the desire in life eleven to bring eternal truth to the West. This is the desire which is to be consummated in life fifteen, and most particularly in the present book, in a new synthesis of East and West.

Cardinal, professor, papal nuncio, patron of the arts and sciences, with a mind nearly as big as his stomach, he however *uses* only his intellect; his heart remains closed. Faith and reason are twin pillars which can be juxtaposed but never combined. Subtle experience does not unite them, nor can ontological depth harmonise them. This life – of intellectual and physical travel (from mind to spirit and West to East) – also determines the location of the next life in Japan, which sets up the reverse journey from East to West from which this book takes its title.

Thus in life seven we see him in Japan as a warlord in a family of warlords, a grand strategist, but with a terrible and fiery temper. If there is a negative *karma* of abuse it is incurred in this life, but is also 'fated' in the sense that he is born into a feudal society characterised by conflict, destruction and death, in which only the strongest survive. Gradually, however, under the patient counsel of one of his generals who practises Zen, he comes to see that there are gentler, simpler and calmer ways of being and doing (accomplishing things). The symbol of this life is the sun, which sets up a poignant echo of the Essene life with its very different tone.

In its next life the soul is born as a woman to a peasant family in China. At a young age she is sold by her father into a richer household. She grows up without education and is used and abused by this new household for profit. She works in a sweatshop making pens and pencils, brushes and ink (an irony for a writer, for whom such things are normally presupposed), cooks and cleans, and tends the pigs, wild boar and other domestic animals of the household. After some time her erstwhile suitor and abuser readily begins to rent her out to other men, attracted by her beauty and industry, for their pleasure. Finding only intermittent refuge in a love affair which had begun in this way, she eventually dies of exhaustion in her mid-forties. This life, like life three, shows the suppression and suffering, but also the strength, of womankind.

In life nine the soul is reborn as a male, again in China but further west – in Szechwan province. Naive, vulnerable and somewhat effeminate (infused with *yin* energy), he leaves home and his mandarin parents at an early age, having been well schooled in all the systems of Chinese philosophy, to write poetry and fathom the mysteries of the universe. But he finds himself scorned for his radical and naturalist Taoist philosophy (into which he wishes to inject an element of spirituality and openness). Abused and neglected, he travels throughout the Chinese world, finding solace only in nature, dreams of a beautiful woman and occasional conversations with sympathetic Buddhist monks. This life, like lives five and eight, is about rejection, the abuse of power but also, like life five, the opening of the heart *chakra*. This is the first life of enlightenment. But though the Chinese poet has the truth, there is no one to hear it. He dies young, lost in contemplation of the beauty of a rose reflected in water (depicted on the cover of the book).

In life ten he moves across the borders to Tibet. He enters a Buddhist monastery at a young age and becomes adept at the techniques of meditation and mindfulness. In contrast to life nine, he here experiences acceptance, gaining recognition and begins to instigate reforms in the theory and practice of Mahayana and Vajrayana Buddhism. The figure of the Buddha meditating high above the Himalayas, but beating close to his heart, is a constant presence in this life, as it will occur in other lives as well. Though his third eye and crown *chakra* are open, he again experiences frustration, this time at the rigidities of the theory and practice of the various monastic orders. He longs for the freedom of spirit and expression of the Indian sages he has met, who are apparently free to say, think and do anything they please.

So he reincarnates in India under the sign of Krishna. He has indeed already had many Indian lives, including one as a pious peasant, another as a temple dancer and a third as a neophyte in an ashram. But in this life he is destined to become a guru with his own ashram. A massive consciousness, he instigates various reforms within the Hindu corpus on the basis of his own original studies of Vedic philosophy. He wishes for religious and political transformation, and criss-crosses the country debating inside and outside his ashram with other gurus on the need for truth and change. As a spiritual teacher of considerable renown he has a massive following, holding a huge swathe of Hindu India in the palm of his hand, but he realises that there is little he can do against the growing power of the West without a spiritual, cultural and intellectual revolution. And so he forms the intention on his deathbed to teach Vedic truth to the West (and in so doing renounces the scorn in which he is held it since his Far Eastern lives). This desire sets up the remaining rounds of lives of the book and can be completed only when he becomes a successful and recognised philosopher in the West, so that he can then, like Moses, take both East and West to the promised land, crossing the Rubicon to a world of abundance without scarcity, of fulfilment without suffering, the immanentisation of heaven on earth.

To do this, however, he must first come to terms with the world of wealth and power, sexuality and money and the boundaries that delineate the physical world from which he has become so detached. He is thus born as a sultan, spending his days alternating between the pleasures of life in his harem with his twenty-eight wives or concubines – one for each day of the lunar cycle – and of his innumerable horses or racing camels, or dispensing arbitrary justice throughout his land. He counts his treasure chest, replete with gold and laced with glittering jewels, several times a week. It grows, as does his land and his power, and his women and his male slaves, which he treats alike as means to his ends. Yet, as he ages, he develops a craving for music and dancing, and in his favorite dancer he begins to find the magic of a different kind of transcendence as his *kundalini* energy starts to flow upwards again. He reads and dances with the Sufi poets and musicians. He begins to radiate a different kind of spirit before he dies. He wishes to see the world unified in the spirit of joy and justice.

But first the *karma* of this life must be played out. Born in southern Italy, near Amalfi, he is endowed with a huge mind but experiences a life of suffering and desire. His throat *chakra* is blocked. He is unable to express himself properly in his speech or in anything he does. He has no resources. With his peasant wife he ekes out a meagre existence, seeing the rich and famous (some of them his former slaves) prosper at his and his kind's expense. He dies young, a Sparticist.

This sets the theme for a Western life of a better-off lifestyle, but also of a distinctly mystical bent. A university professor and prolific writer, he is also a mystic in love with nature (especially the stars – astrologically not just astronomically), a doctor concerned with new ways of (self) healing, a political revolutionary who believes in the possibility of a society without money and one which would satisfy the ideals of primitive communism. Born of diplomatic parents, he is educated by a stern governess from whom he quickly grows free. He travels widely, is fluent with languages and interested in all aspects of the revolutions of modernity. He travels to America and Russia, deriding both. He is a naturalist who believes in angels and fairies. He has much in common with the Chinese philosopher of life nine as well as the Ancient Greek of life two. Moreover, if the emphasis in life six is on the left brain, the intellect, here it is balanced by recognition of the co-equal importance of the right brain, intuition. Interested in the phenomena that can only be revealed by an open third eye, he begins to see his mission, completed in life fifteen, to be that of a synthesis of East and West.

[The Aquarian Age]

Born in London in 1944 of an Indian father and an English mother, his task is to reconcile and resynthesise the opposites: East and West, male and female, *yin* and *yang*, reason and experience, fact and value, mind and body, heaven and earth, they aspectually embody. Abused as a young child, he suffers a miserable childhood, despite his theosophical upbringing. Finally he flees home with an Oxford scholarship to study philosophy, politics and economics, against his father's wishes. He gains honour after honour, but with each original twist in his life and thought he suffers the rejection of the system. He achieves all the goals he sets for himself. He eventually becomes as radical and revolutionary as it is possible to get in Western philosophical terms, until materialism is transcended in the context of a global philosophy, both perennially old and radically new. It is this perennial philosophy for the new millenium which this very book initiates. The means and end is enlightenment, and universal human emancipation is seen to be a condition of planetary survival. This life also becomes one of integration of some of the insights of the New Age and the New Left movements.

Life fifteen sees the integration of the *chakra* system, fulfilling the desire of life eleven and realising the goal of life nine on the basis of the inspirations afforded by Jesus in life five, Moses in life one, Pythagoras in life two, Buddha in life ten, Krishna in life eleven, and many others in life after life. Each life is connected with a different colour or *chakra* or complex of colours or *chakras*. Each life is karmically connected to the lives preceding and following it. The sequence of lives is completed only when the desire for desire, the cause of all suffering, is relinquished.

I

GENERAL THEORETICAL INTRODUCTION

FROM CRITICAL REALISM TO THE PHILOSOPHY OF SELF-REALISATION

My aim in this general theoretical introduction is to work systematically through the four moments or levels of dialectical critical realism, as briefly described in the introduction to the book (namely 1M of ontology, 2E of absence, 3L of totality and 4D of transformative agency or creative work) in order to show how the dialectic of critical realism at once prepares the ground for and necessitates its development into the *transcendental* dialectical critical realism or philosophy of (universal) Self-realisation (and ultimately of God-realisation) espoused in the present work and which theoretically underpins the narrative of *From East to West*. I shall spend relatively longer on 1M, treating in particular the topic of ontology, dispositional realism (and the stratification of being, including emergence and disemergence), categorial realism and philosophy, and the nature of God and transcendence, not only because this is an indispensable (and not well understood) ground for the developments at 2E–4D essayed here, but also because the developments at 2E (aside from the critique of Hegelian dialectic), such as the duality of absence, the deduction (which turns on the emergent powers of intentional states) of the trio of reincarnation, *karma* and *moksha* (liberation), the dialectic of and in *From East to West* and the dialectical critique of analytical reason (which paves the way for the critique of standard conceptions of the subject and the self); at 3L, such as the nature of identity, the self, totality and holistic (heterocosmic, reflexive and other 'non-linear' or quantised) causality; and at 4D, such as the nature of *dharma* (which links the 3L critique of the self to 4D agency) and spontaneous right action, the dialectics of self-realisation (which also involves centrally disemergence), the character of the social cube in the context of the physical embodiment of human being and the relations between East and West, are themselves topicalised or at least clearly exemplified in the dialectical narrative of the book. I shall start then with 1M, the realm of ontology and realism, truth and God.

1 1M: Ontology

1.1 On ontology

The foremost claims of the transcendental realism essayed in *A Realist Theory of Science* are (1) to have established the *irreducibility* of ontology or the theory of being to epistemology or the theory of knowledge and a fortiori (and against the epistemic fallacy) that of being to knowledge, of being to our (i.e. human) knowledge of being; and (2) to have demonstrated some propositions in it, that is, to have given the re-vindicated subject of ontology a certain *content* or *shape*. Ontology is of course necessary for any self-conscious and consistent realism, and its defence is therefore essential for combating the various scepticisms noted in the foreword. Moreover, the fact that I argue not only for its possibility and necessity (indeed inexorability) but also for its possessing a definite content – that is, not only for being, but for the contours or shape of being (and for their necessity too) – is of the utmost moment. For it is in the last instance what distinguishes transcendental realism from transcendental idealism, and all the traditions that stem from or invoke it (however repugnant they might have been to its founder), including contemporary discourse theory[1] and a whole host of currently fashionable modern and postmodern positions. In particular, following my present rethematisation of ontology and its consequences (in the present section), I want to argue, as already posted, for a dispositional (including transfactual, stratified and emergentist) realism in section 1.2, a categorial (conceptual, constellational and meta-philosophical) realism in section 1.3 and a realism about transcendence, the transcendent (both in the sense of the beyond and in the sense of the unbounded) and especially God in section 1.4 as a necessary part or necessary features of the shape of being.

It is important to note that *ontological realism* is not only consistent with but also entails epistemological, and more generally experiential, *relativism*, including pluralism, diversity and fallibilism; so that we can allow that God, or the absolute, or the transcendent (or transcendent beings or phenomena generally) can, like nature (or ordinary material things), be accessed or experienced in a multiplicity of different ways. This is, moreover, quite consistent with a moment of *judgemental rationalism* in the intrinsic or normative aspect of the transitive or epistemological and social, relative, dimension of science (see *SRHE* C1 and elsewhere). Judgemental rationalism in turn is not the same as *judgementalism,* which is prescriptively and abstractly universalising and derives, at least in part, from the failure to acknowledge the *concrete singularity* of the *dharma* (nature, station or

1 see my debate with Ernesto Laclau in *Alethia 1.2* (1998).

position) of the individual, group or situation concerned, and the objectively grounded but specific and possibly unique rationality and morality flowing from it (that *dharma*).

The arguments for ontology are classifiable into at least four overlapping kinds (but there will also be many other types, and accordingly taxonomies):

1 Arguments from the presuppositions of *any* human being, or at least *most* human beings, as we know it, including from:

   i discourse;
   ii desire and the whole host of other affective states, and indeed intentional states generally;
   iii agency;
   iv perception.[2]

2 Arguments from the conditions of possibility of an array of *everyday* activities, from making a cup of coffee to finding and fixing a fault in a machine (see *DPF* C3.1).
3 Arguments from the conditions of possibility of *particular forms* of human experience – for example, religious or aesthetic experience – but most momentously perhaps from those of
3' *science*, and in particular from (a) experimental activity (see *RTS* C1.3B) and (b) the possibility (and actuality) of scientific change and difference (see my *Reclaiming Reality* (London: Verso 1989) C3, pp. 32–3).
4 Arguments from the *auto-subversive* nature of texts or discourses that are anti-ontological or at least agnostic about ontology (which are similar to arguments of type 1.i above).

All these species of argument not only establish the legitimacy and irreducibility of ontology but, also articulate a certain content or contours for it, that is, impart to ontology substance and shape. So we need to ask: what kind of world (what shape to being) does a form of activity presuppose or some particular theory postulate or imply? For an ontology of some kind is *inexorable*, a presupposition of everything we do and an implication of everything we say. The question is not *whether* to do ontology or not, but *what* ontology it is that one does. The only 'whethers' in this neck of the woods are whether one's ontology is explicit or implicit, that is, whether it is self-conscious, and whether it can be rationally justified.[3]

2 For i–iii, see *DPF* C3.1, and for iv, see *RTS* C1.3A.
3 Thus nothing is more significant than the way in which an anti-ontologist such as Habermas tacitly secretes

Let us consider possibly the simplest consideration or argument for ontology, from discourse (1.i). The procedure which I have called 'referential detachment', that is, the detachment of the act of reference from that to which it refers, establishes at once the existential separation, distinctiveness or 'intransitivity' of both referential act and referent and the possibility of another reference to either, a condition of any intelligible discourse at all.[4]

Ontology, then, is implicit in all language use (as indeed it is in all intentional action). In particular to deny it (see arguments of type 4 above) is to commit performative contradiction (4D). That is, referential detachment and hence existential intransitivity and thence ontology (1M) – and ontology of a specific (here minimally bi-polar, thence multi-polar, processual and so on) type – is necessary to sustain the intelligibility of the discursive act by which ontology (reality, being and so on) is denied.[5]

The result is that the anti-ontologist fails to satisfy the (4D) *reflexive* criterion for a philosophy, that it should be capable of situating or sustaining itself and its own aefficacy. Moreover it fails to satisfy this criterion by *alienating* (3L), hypostatising or otherwise excluding philosophy, or at least the particular discursive act in which ontology is denied, from the world or reality (totality) it is talking about (and thence within). But to hypostatise or otherwise effectively exclude a (and often all) discourse is *paradoxically*[6] (and, if the discourse is *also* or includes that by which it is excluded, *auto-subversively*) to deny it any causal aefficacy in that world, and so undermines its point or rationale, or even the possibility of its being understood. For this presupposes at least the possibility of its having a

a positivist ontology of nature in his epistemological elaboration of our knowledge-constitutive interest in prediction and control (*Knowledge and the Human Interests*, London, 1972). This interest, it transpires, turns precisely on the Humean theory of causal laws and the Popper–Hempel model of explanation, which presupposes a deductivist world of invariant regularities (or constant conjunctions), actualist and closed (flat and finished). Ontology is presupposed in the gesture, that is, the elaboration of the very theory, in which it is denied.

4 It is important for the theme of this introduction to note that with the first act of referential detachment comes the first possibility of *attachment* (whether in the positive form of desire or the negative form of aversion or fear), crucially linking or indexing the reference to the chain of *avidya* and the web of *maya* already outlined in the introduction to the book. Intransitivity, *duality* and polarity, characteristic of all relative or dependent being, must, however, be differentiated from alienation, *dualism* and split, which are specific to mystified or 'demi-real' modes of relative being. (If absolute being is characterised by *identity* and relative being by *unity*, demi-real being is by *alienation*.) The desideratum for relative being is *action* (including referential action), not without discrimination, but rather *without attachment*. And, as we shall see, this presupposes an ethic of *unconditional love*. For conditional love just is (or implies) attachment.

5 For what is it that is said or done but something that *is* (a being or existent)? That is, unless the anti-ontological argument occurred, i.e. *was*, in which case it is (or was) real, there is nothing to argue about or over; and if it did, the case for ontology has been tacitly conceded.

6 This is paradoxical – paradox is one of the forms of oppositionality characteristic of the chain of *avidya* (*PE*, pp. 242–3) – because normally (or at least nominally) idealistic irrealism entails excluding ideas or

(minimally necessary) effect, and so being (minimally) effective, which presupposes, since causal aefficacy is the most general criterion for reality, its *being* in the totality in and to which it is addressed (and thence about). So we have a (2E) *split* or dichotomy or dualism, between philosophy or discourse and the rest of reality, most characteristically related to and indeed resting upon the reason/cause and mind/body dualisms. At the root of both are the paradoxical and auto-subversive denial of the causal *explicability*, *aefficacy* and *emergence* of intentional states (such as that of the *attachment* which binds human beings to the cycle of *reincarnation*, governed by *karmic* causality, or of its cessation upon which *moksha* or liberation depends). All these (progressively deeper) categorial errors embed the discourse or thought in (progressively deeper) chains of absence–*avidya*–*maya* (including myopic attachment, instrumental reasoning and reification (and thence into undialectical – for example, exclusively analytical and abstract, and so incorrect – thought and action) and conditionality (and thence into the cycle of rebirth, *karma* and heteronomy or unfreedom))–dualism, alienation, *tina* formation and heteronomous (supplementary) determination, rooted in the self-alienation of human beings.

The critical realist, then, can allow that discourse is a reality but argues against the 'linguistic fallacy' that there are other realities besides discourse which can be referred to in (as the referent of) discourse. Many of these realities exist independently of discourse (as well as the discursive act in which they are picked out). Moreover, irrespective of whether or not they do so, some of their referents may, and arguably must, be apprehended pre-linguistically, or more generally extra-linguistically.

The original argument establishing the ontology of transcendental realism was of type 3'a, a transcendental argument from experimental activity (*RTS* C1.3B) in which it was shown that the radically non-Humean, stratified, differentiated and open nature of reality was a condition of the possibility of experimental, but equally also (*RTS* C2) of applied scientific activity. In particular, a disjunction was established between the domains of the real, actual and empirical, such that the domain of the real contains but is not exhausted by the domain of the actual, which in turn contains but is not exhausted by the domain of the empirical – which may be written as $d_r \geq d_a \geq d_e$ (see *RTS* C1.6).

language from the rest of reality, while urging their priority. By the same token (irrealist) materialists find it difficult to sustain the aefficacy and power of their own rhetoric, or of ideas in general. At the root of both is a dualistic separation of mind or ideas and material being and a denial of the emergence of intentional states as explicable and aefficacious parts of reality. Conversely realism, as we shall see, allows us to reassess the role of ideas, texts and so on (including philosophical ones) in geo-history, including their material objectification and embodiment (as technology) in socialised nature, as tools and artefacts, machines and computers, but also as causally aefficacious in constituting and cementing the structures of social life.

The *philosophical ontologies* explicitly articulated by such arguments, or otherwise tacitly presupposed, delineate the general character, contours or shape of being, or we could say (as we shall see in section 1.3 below) they explicate its categorial structure. They must be distinguished from the specific *scientific ontologies* constituted by particular scientific theories, postulating particular types of entities and processes, which detail the specific features and particular contents of the general landscape which the philosophical ontology demarcates and charts.

The argument demonstrating the irreducibility of (potentially knowable) causal laws to recorded empirical regularities in experimentally or otherwise closed systems (and hence the stratification, transfactuality, emergence and so on (see section 1.2 below) of both nature, more generally being, and our knowledge of it) establishes at once the propriety and irreducibility (and thence inevitability) of ontology and its content and a fortiori of its subject matter, being (which contains human knowledge as a proper subset). Underlying the epistemic fallacy and the reduction of being (which includes but is not exhaustive of knowledge, language and so on) to known being is a widespread *anthropic fallacy*, namely the reduction or analysis of *being* to or in terms of purely *human being*, of which the linguistic fallacy, the analysis of being in terms of purely human language, is normally a variant.

A corollary of the inevitability of ontology is that its denial, as we have already seen, leads to the secretion of an implicit ontology, so that we have reflexive inconsistency, denegation, *tina* formation and the generation or emergence of heteronomous orders of determination. And with it we have intrication into a characteristic chain of a more or less specific type of *avidya* (error) and *maya* (illusion), generated by normatively negative absence (incompleteness or lack), and entraining dualism (split), alienation, reification, performative contradiction and so on. But if the shape or content as well as the subject of ontology is necessary, then for each aspect or feature of the necessary shape of being omitted from or misdescribed in the implicit ontology secreted by an irrealist account, that account will intricate progressively deeper chains of *avidya*, which in this way form an interlocking web or meshwork. That is to say, if transcendental (as distinct from say empirical or conceptual) realism – or at a deeper level, dialectical critical realism (or even, as I argue it is, TDCR) – is transcendentally and so categorially and hence axiologically necessary, then, at that deeper level and in the appropriate respect and degree of specificity, it (or some specific feature of it) will perforce need to be tacitly presupposed, so generating a series of deeper and more specific levels of implicit ontology and realism, initiating further levels or rounds of performative contradiction, dualism (split), alienation, reification, *tina* formation and heteronomous (supplementary) determination.

Reification occurs here as an inevitable corollary of alienation, itself the product of *avidya* or categorial error and the illusion or *maya* it generates. What is alienated or excluded from consciousness is tacitly secreted, unconsciously presupposed and so, though dependent upon – and only *in virtue of* – conscious human activity, it cannot be treated as such. The implicit ontology, realism (critical realism) and so on is so held in an unreflected and un-self-conscious, unstated, mode. It appears, when necessary, as a kind of Derridean supplement, a symptom of categorial incompleteness or lack, in some *tina* compromise formation.

But the reification *of* ontology merely reflects the reification *within* it, as when, for instance our human knowledge of (transfactually and so independently aefficacious) causal laws is seen as occurring independently of the cognitive and practical human activity necessary to establish them. I have argued (in *RR* C4 and *SRHE* C3) that the *reification* of knowledge is coupled on to the *anthropocentricity* – and ultimately *egocentricity* – of existing philosophical ontology, and philosophy generally; and that they mutually entail and support each other, most typically in the duplicitous exchanges of subject–object identity theories (see *DPF passim*). Conversely, progress in philosophy depends upon (or essentially involves movement towards) greater self→Self-consciousness.

This development – from egocentricity to Self-consciousness – is of course an aspect of the dialectic of self-realisation which this book describes and this introduction thematises. At the same time we are now in a position to begin to trace a general pattern in the *dialectic of maya* (of which the denegation of ontology is a form). Objectively (or indeed subjectively) constituted *illusion*, itself grounded in categorial error (*avidya*) and incompleteness, generates substantive *error* (mistakes, misjudgements, incorrect actions), which generates *fear*. This in turn generates *attachment* (a defence against fear of loss or *not getting*, or more generally failure), conditionality, instrumental reasoning, reification, heteronomous determination and so on. And attachment causes *suffering*, unhappiness which is quickly transferred on to others in the guise of *oppression* (accordingly, spreading suffering) and other modes of ill-being. It is myopic to attempt to eliminate suffering without first attending to its causes. (This is the great teaching of the Buddha over two and a half millennia ago.)

1.2 Dispositional realism

I now want to argue for the *irreducibility* of the possible to the actual, of being to doing (behaviour) and of the self to agency; and to affirm the ontological, epistemological and logical *priority* of the first over the second term in each case. What I am calling 'dispositional realism' is suggested by aspects of the four recent turns in contemporary thought I mentioned in the introduction to the book; and the move to more realist, processual, holistic and reflexive (or self-referential) ways of thinking (and being) is also associated with a more energetic (and ecological), as well as transcendental and self-conscious (and thence emancipatory) conception of being.

A disposition is basically a power, and to say that something S *has* (or perhaps just *is*) the power to do x is to say that even when S does x, it does it *ceteris paribus* in virtue of its intrinsic nature, *if* it does it at all (i.e. though it is contingent whether it ever does so). But I shall be working with a very broad concept of disposition. This embraces capacities, properties, powers, liabilities, affordances, tendencies, fields, rights, duties and so on. Moreover it is consistent with (1) a wide variety of different types of conditions (for the exercise of the power) and groundings (in intrinsic natures) and (2) both qualitative and quantitative descriptions, including probabilistic and statistical ones. In the latter case the traditional concept of a mass event, i.e. a mass or collectivity of undifferentiated or punctiform events, must be differentiated from the holistic or quantum concept of an *event itself* as a mass, collectivity or *totality* – to take a simple example, as a distribution or spread in space, or a succession or flow in time, or both – a rhythmic matrix in space–time.[7] In general the dispositionalist, as distinct from actualist, orientation focuses on *internal*, as distinct from external, *totalising* as distinct from atomistic or punctual, *necessary* as distinct from contingent, and *subjective* as distinct from object-oriented determinations.

I want to demonstrate the necessity for a three-tier (possibility, exercise, actualisation), in contrast to the more conventional two-tier (grounding, manifestation), analysis of dispositions. And I am going to argue for the necessity of dispositional realism:

A for the analysis of causal laws, and in ontology generally (establishing the irreducibility of powers to their exercise and of their exercise to any particular actualised outcome);

B in indicating the direction and sustaining the essential dynamic of scientific discovery, from manifest phenomena to the underlying structures which generate them, moving always in a direction of greater depth or totality of being; and,

C in explicating not only a necessary phase of knowledge but also any and all conceivable limits to knowledge – and indeed being generally, in what I have labelled 'ultimata' – which are characterised by a *dispositional identity*, i.e. an identity between a being and its causal powers, whether they are changing or not, and whether they are being exercised or not.

In terms of (A), transcendental realism establishes that a constant conjunction of

7 Compare the shift in biological thinking from the idea of an organism as an individual to the idea of it as a genetically endowed *individual-in-its-*(developing)*-environment* (or *Umwelt*).

events is neither (1) sufficient nor (2) necessary for the operation of a causal law. (1) It cannot be sufficient, because of the well-known aporiai, such as the problem of induction (see *RTS* C3.5–6) and the chains of *avidya–tina* formation these aporiai entrain – which arise from assuming it is; so that the powers of things (structures and totalities) cannot be reduced to their manifestation in a sequence of events. (2) But neither can it be necessary. For causal laws, and the generative mechanisms and structures located in the nature of the things which explain them, continue to operate in open systems, where they are exercised without being actualised or manifest in a particular outcome. Hence they must be analysed *transfactually* as the exercise of the powers of things which, while causally aefficacious, co-determining the phenomena of the world, may be exercised without being realised in any particular, let alone regular, way at all.[8]

That is to say, then, the exercise of causal laws shows that science presupposes a philosophical ontology on which the powers of beings (entities, structures, fields, totalities including ultimata) can be *possessed* without being *exercised* and exercised without being *actualised* in any particular outcome, let alone whether they are *experienced* (perceived or otherwise detected) by science (or human beings generally). Powers, exercise and actualisation constitute the three tiers of the analysis of dispositions.

Moving on to (B) and thence (C), scientific knowledge is characteristically *stratified* and science must be seen as a *process in motion*, always on the move from manifest phenomena to explanatory structures, located at a deeper or broader (more encompassing) level of totality, which must then in turn be described and explained. In this process, science develops through distinctive Humean, Kantian, Lockean and Leibnizian phases, in a dialectic driven by contradictions (inconsistencies) and anomalies and so on, induced by absence (incompleteness) and remedied by the creative discovery of new levels or dimensions of reality.

The basic structure of the logic of that scientific discovery[9] is this. Given an (say, experimentally generated) event regularity, or an apparently non-random pattern in nature, scientists seek a mechanism or process, grounded in the intrinsic nature or real essence of the thing or totality concerned, which, if it existed, would explain why it behaved the way it did. Once the relevant mechanism has been identified, scientists seek to explain *it* in terms of the nature of the thing which grounds it. This is in principle empirically discoverable and describable. And when it has been described, scientists go on to explain it (driven once

8 As the *Bhagavad Gita* says, the actual course of nature – though not its (real, deep, underlying) structure – is unfathomable. Among the reasons for its unpredictability are free will and the multiplicity and variety of agencies, determinations and constraints; so that the operation, though not the form, of karmic laws cannot be predetermined before the action occurs, i.e. the *karma* is initiated.

9 I first described this in *RTS* C3; see also *DPF* C3.2.

more by incompleteness) in terms of deeper and/or wider levels of being. It follows from this both (1) that analytic a posteriori knowledge is possible and (2) that the categorial clause implicit in a dispositional or powers-type statement plays, contrary to charges familiar since the time of Molière and Hume, a key role in indicating or expressing the logic of the essential direction of scientific research: from actualised, manifest phenomena to the real (potentially unmanifest) powers and possibilities of the things (powers which may, and, at the level of ultimata, must constitute them) which, when exercised, in complex and variegated ways, explain them.

From this perspective, the *stratification* of scientific knowledge reflects the *real stratification* of being. In general, if:

1 a more basic (deeper or wider) level A *explains* a less basic, dependent or higher order, more immediately manifest, already-known level B, then A typically provides only the *enabling* or affordance conditions, the conditions of possibility for B. A does not determine B, though it is a determination of B. The *selection* conditions are self-determined by B; and/or other layers or levels, moments or agencies of determination circumscribe, overlay or are inscribed within B.[10]

2 B, the higher-order level is – or at least may be – synchronically or diachronically *emergent* from A (see *RTS* C2.5, *DPF* C2.2).[11] In particular,

3 B is normally causally and taxonomically irreducible to A (see *SRHE*, p. 113); that is, reference to B is necessary to explain states of B and perhaps some states of A, although not A's intrinisic nature.[12]

4 B is normally[13] unilaterally existentially dependent on A, which could, and may, exist without B but not vice versa.[14] Moreover, typically B will not only be existentially dependent on, but partly existentially constituted by, A. So that we may say,

5 A is *ontologically ingredient* in, but does not *exhaust* B, i.e. it is only *part* of the substance or stuff of B. (This follows from B's emergence.) Note that this

10 This allows us to see how *free will* and relative autonomy are consistent with constraint and ultimate determination, on which more anon.

11 Correlatively disemergence occurs with the removal or disconnection of B, and may take the form of liberation from a degree of constraint on freedom, for example from illusory and other heteronomous modes or orders of determination and constraint.

12 It is on this feature of emergent (intentional) states that, as we shall see in section 2, the transcendental deduction of the ideas of reincarnation and *karma* depend.

13 Except for some special geo-historically emergent contexts or totalities characterised by situations, relations or structures of co-dependence; see below.

14 A may, but in general will not be an ultimatum; and if it is an ultimatum, it may or may not be absolute, i.e. independent or autonomous; again, see below.

6 Ontological immanence or ingredience of A in B is quite consistent with its epistemic or experiential transcendence. For A was not initially known, and may not even have been manifest, in the context of the dialectics of scientific discovery described; and it both pre-exists and endures through our knowledge of it, at least in its essential nature, although not necessarily in its specific states.[15] Finally, note that A contains or includes – I shall say *constellationally* (see *DPF* C2.7) contains or includes – i.e. overreaches – B, in virtue of its greater depth and/or extension – generally, totality – of being. Thus,

7 A constellationally contains but is not saturated (or exhausted) by (i.e. it is neither co-intensive or co-extensive with) B, in virtue of both its greater totality (depth and width, extension) and its independence.

On the dispositional realist account, the world is constituted by often intersecting levels or networks of being of ever-increasing wholeness, ultimately circumscribed (if it is circumscribed at all) by an absolute of potentially limitless depth and/or extension.[16]

(C) ultimata, characterised by dispositional identity, may be *real* or merely *epistemic* (i.e. given our present knowledge, for the moment, for us). They may be local, regional or total (i.e. complete, whole), enduring or transient, potential or actualised, quiescent (latent, dormant) or active. Non-ultimate levels of being are dependent or *relative*. Ultimate levels of being are more or less *relatively absolute* or relatively independent. Non-relatively *absolute* or completely independent being (the real, total and enduring ultimatum) or the *absolute* simpliciter is God. God is the alethic or the ultimate (self-grounded) ground of all grounds of being, the unconditioned condition of possibility of all conditions and all possibilities. God as *unmanifest* is an absolute ground of pure dispositionality; as *manifest* is so, (a) in realised beings, that is beings who are (or so I shall argue) at one with their categorial essence or real nature (and free from extraneous determination), and (b) in other, unrealised beings only partially, mediately and heteronomously, yet still as, despite this, however, their ultimate ground and telos.

But the absolute may itself be relativised in a number of significant ways. Most obviously, it may be a merely, in-itself (intrinsically) dependent absolute, only an absolute-for-us: that is, a relative absolute, or an absolute relativised (restricted)

15 It is this feature of the stratification of being which allows us to reconcile the ontological immanence and transcendence of God.

16 That is to say an absolute which is constituted by a degree, potentially unknowable to us, from our cosmic standpoint, of potentially limitless (transfinite) series of levels or degrees of limitlessness or unboundedness. Note that this consideration entails that if the limitless is 'without limitation', i.e. *omnipotent* (as in traditional characterisations of the absolute or of God), then we may have to think the concept of degrees or orders of omnipotence.

to our zone of being; or a relative absolute in the sense of a human epistemic or experiential one. However even the realm of the intrinsically absolute (-in-itself, and not just-for-us, so to speak), that is, completely independent or autonomous being, may be characterised by relations of internal dependency or (what is not necessarily the same thing) different degrees or orders of autonomy, self-sufficiency or independence. Most interestingly, perhaps, the absolute, as already indicated, may be constituted by a potentially infinite series of potentially rankable hierarchies of levels of limitlessness, unboundedness, omnipotence (or infinity!). That is to say, autonomy, totality, omnipotence, unboundedness may all (though not in the same way, and not perhaps by us) be *both* qualitatively and/or quantitatively differentiatable *and* unbounded or infinite in depth and extent, intensity and scope.

Inscribed within relative (dependent) human being are levels of *false dependent* (relative) being or *demi-reality* (illusory, veiled, occluded, twilight, demi-being, so to speak). So far, then, we have a sequence of:

1 (possible degrees or orders of) *absolute* being;
2 various modalities of *relatively absolute* being;
3 *relative* (dependent) *being*; including
3' *relative* (dependent) *human* being; and
4 *demi-real* (illusory or false, dependent relative human) being.

The schema may be completed in two ways. The first is by distinguishing (a) *objectively constituted* demi-real being – the web of *maya* or objective illusion – within which a discrimination between veridical and non-veridical perception and judgement may be made, from (b) *purely subjective* errors and illusions, so as to give us a category or class of:

5 purely *subjective false dependent being*.[17]

It is important to stress here that independent, relative and illusory being (whether of types 4 or 5) are all alike real, i.e. exist and so are contained, like everything, within the subject matter of ontology. Moreover, as such, they are all potentially and to a degree actually causally aefficacious, although differentially so.

Second, the schema is completed in practice, as I have already noted, by the diachronic emergence of various synchronic relations of (frequently asymmetrically charged) *co-dependence*, so that we have

17 Illusion (in being, in the intransitive dimension) one could say is no illusion (error) or delusion (of judgement, in the transitive dimension), but exists and is ubiquitous and aefficacious in the self-alienated social world. Objective illusion is of course ultimately subjectively grounded in the self-alienation of man.

which may hold either within or between the other classes or orders of this 'ladder of being'.

Finally, it should be stressed that in the hierarchy of being, a more basic level provides only the conditions of possibility and impossibility of the more dependent, and at least within the stratification of relative being, emergent level. It follows from this that its dependence is always relative; and that 'determination' is never (or at least very rarely), as normally understood, 'determinism' (*RTS* C2 *passim*).

1.3 Categorial realism

In the introduction to the book, I argued that the alienations and malaises in contemporary thought – *conceptual alienations* – were to be explained in terms of the *real alienations* and ills of people in their social settings in (generalised) four-planar social being; and that this in turn was to be explained in terms of the *self-alienation* of men and women. Subject to the qualifications already expressed, and in particular recognition of the fact that not only the concept of the self but also selves themselves are elastic, expanding and developing, we can simplify the character of this self-alienation by thematising it along two dimensionalities: alienation of human beings from their Self or soul, producing *inner* conflict and alienation; and alienation of human beings from their social–natural Totality (including the structures of four-planar social life), and ultimately the cosmos, producing *outer* conflict and alienation (both *between* the individual and the totality and *within* the totality extrinsic to him), ecological as well as social. So far in the first two sections of this chapter, I have been developing the ontological infrastructure necessary to think the possibility of transcending this self-alienation in a dialectic of Self-realisation (which will also be self- (or ego-) transcendence), ultimately in universal Self-realisation or 'unity existence'.

My aim in the present sub-section is to develop a robust realism about *categories* (traditionally regarded as defining the province of philosophy) as a prolegomenon to the next, when I argue that God is the ultimate categorial structure of the world, including human beings, which are essentially but not only *Godly* (or Godlike), a feature they have forgotten and from which they have become alienated (an index of their self-alienation).

Under the influence of Kant and others, a subjectivist account of categories, as essentially interpretative schemes or taxonomic (classificatory) devices imposed by human beings upon the world, as essentially human-dependent, has become prevalent. But for critical realism categories such as causality, substance, process, totality, agency and so on are essentially constitutive (albeit very abstract or skeletal) features of the world, defining precisely its most basic properties or ingredients (which is what the ontology of DCR purports to begin to do). Causality, absence, space, time, emergence and so on are all real features of being. This is the only position consistent with a *transcendental* realism. Would it not be absurd to, for example, hold that causal laws existed and acted independently of human beings but not causality or natural lawfulness? This would be akin to being a realist about knives, forks and spoons but not about cutlery. The fact the categories cannot be *known* as categories before human beings does not mean that they do not *exist* as such before them. To suppose otherwise is precisely to commit the epistemic fallacy. And it is precisely the categorial or most fundamental constitutive structures of reality (those without which other structures of the world could not exist) that transcendental realism (as further developed by (transcendental) dialectical critical realism) begins to delineate.

Realism about being thus includes, and indeed ultimately depends upon, realism about categories – categorial realism – which situates the pre and objectively constituted categorisation of being. Moreover a transitive dimension/intransitive dimension distinction holds between *our* descriptions or accounts of the categories, i.e. our meta-epistemically relative and fallible conceptualisations or categorisations of being (in the transitive (epistemological or social) dimension, or TD) and its real or true categorisation (in the intransitive (ontological) dimension, or ID). Of course our epistemic categorisation is also real, but it is not what it is about, even when it is correct. The epistemic is constellationally contained within being (which also includes the non-extra- and pre-epistemic). Transcendental realism, especially as developed in dialectical critical realism, insists that everything, including logical contradictions, category mistakes and concepts generally (not to mention human actions), is part of being. To exclude *anything* is to alienate it, dualistically split being and so initiate a chain of *avidya–tina* formation. However, neither such a *constellational realism* (realism about everything) nor the *conceptual realism* it entails is what is meant by categorial realism. although all three are features of any self-consistent realism. Categorial realism is more specific, insisting on the transcendental reality of the categories prior to and independently of any knowledge or account of them.

It will help to fix the discussion if we had some examples of social categories in mind. Money, capital, wages, prices, housing, higher education, health care, religious worship and war are all examples of social categories. Differentiating features of social reality from which *inter alia* its emergent and relational properties flow (see *PON* 2.5 and *DPF* C2.9) are:

1 its *conceptuality*, the fact that it is *dependent* upon but not *exhausted* by agents' conceptualisations of the activities in which they engage;

2 its *activity-dependence* (or axiologicality), that it does not exist independently of (although again it is not exhausted by) conscious human agency; and thus
3 it is also dependent on the stratified *nature* of human beings, and the stratification of the (to be here generalised) social totality in which they act (and in which they are at least in part formed).[18]

These three features immediately indicate three modes of *false but dependent* social being – of demi-reality – involving *conceptual absence* and *alienation* and *real* absence and alienation, either *at* a level of social reality or *from* a more basic level underlying it; and a fortiori three ways in which social reality can be *objectively* but *falsely* constituted and so categorised. These demarcate ways in which social reality may contain and even come to be dominated by falsity (*maya*, ideology or objective illusion), modes in which it is untrue respectively *of* (or about) *in* and *to* (or for) itself.

Let us consider these three in turn. Social reality, like natural reality, is really pre-categorised (in the ID) independently of any *account* of its categorial constitution or categorisation (in the TD). However it follows from the conceptuality of social reality that it may be falsely but objectively (although dependently) categorised by agents; and that that illusory categorisation – in ideological discourse – will be a real part of the totality it obscures. To spell this out, agents' accounts of the categorisation (fundamental constitutive structure) of the social reality they inhabit may be:

a false (in the TD), i.e. inadequate to its object (in the ID), which it may veil, distort or otherwise occlude; but be
b a pre-existing and objectively constituted (that is, independently of the subjects perception of it) and causally aefficacious[19] *part* of social reality, lived as a conceptualised moment in its reproduction or transformation, and which is nevertheless
c (generally unilaterally (see 1.2 above) within the stratification of social reality), dependent for its existence and power, i.e. aefficacy, on the true categorial structure it misdescribes and obscures.

This gives us at least two levels of categorisation of being. But there may be false as well as true accounts (or descriptions) of the false categorisation of being, and a

18 Of course there is stratification (including arguably conceptual stratification) prior to the level of the most underlying real essence or intrinsic nature of human beings, or of social totalities. Moreover stratification is polyadic, not dyadic. (See *DPF* 2.7 and *passim*.)

19 So distinguishing it from a purely idiosyncratic, transient or personal subjective interpretation.

multiplicity of false conceptualisations of that level of being, some of both of which may be objectively constituted too, so that demi-reality may be stratified and differentiated. In particular, there may be many aspects or declensions, and layers or levels of ideology or illusion, each generating a characteristic chain (or chains) of *avidya–tina* formation – heteronomous determination. And all may depend upon a (conceptual) absence, the omission of a true description of the categorial structure, which the ideological formation obscures. Note also that there may be no available or currently existing account of the true categorisation (or basic existential constitution) of being, which makes the illusion or lived level of misdescription possible. So, ideology here may resemble the layers of an unpeeled onion or an artichoke.

Typically, what is omitted from an ideological account is an underlying or otherwise deep and/or extensive level of structure at that order or level of reality; and it is in terms of the omission (forgetting, suppression, 'censorship') of the structure that the false (or myopic, superficial, misleading) consciousness is to be explained. But this structure may be self-contradictory, radically incomplete, absurd or otherwise false in itself, as, for instance, is the wage form on Marx's analysis of it (see *PON*, p. 52).[20] Here we have the false constitution of social reality quite independently of any conceptualisation of it, or rather independently of the absence of a true conceptualisation of it (independently, so to speak, of conceptual *avidya*). And typically, it is this mode of real falsity and alienation which will (at least proximately) explain the conceptual alienation just considered, with the latter being closely coupled on to the former.

Before proceeding on to the third mode of objectively constituted false but dependent being, of demi-reality, I want to rehearse the analysis of truth in *DPF*, pp. 217–8. There I showed the necessity for a fourfold analysis of truth, that is, as (1) normative–fiduciary (in the IA); as (2) *adequating* (or we could say epistemic) (in the TD); as (3) *expressive–referential* (as an epistemic–ontic (TD–ID) dual); and as (4) genuinely ontological or *alethic* (in the ID). Corresponding to the distinctions between (2), (3) and (4) we have distinctions between

1' untruth or falsity *about* an object or being (at any one level l_j of reality) (see 1);
2' untruth or falsity *in* an object or being (at that level of reality) (see 2);
3' untruth or falsity of an object or being *to* its essential nature or intrinsic self (see 3),

constituted (in virtue of the stratification of being[21]) by falsity to one or more

20 This, constituted by the absence of such distinctions as between labour and labour power, use value and exchange value and concrete and abstract labour, reflects the real alienation and reification of the worker in capitalist society.

21 Of course, as we have seen, the stratification of being is already implicated in (1). The false account is, so to

basic levels (l_i, l_{i-1}) *ingredient in it* (see 1.2 above), that is, its alethic ground or fundamental categorial structure, its essential nature or its true or, as we say, higher self. In this case the real alienation at a level of reality (2) which explains the conceptual alienation at that level (1) is ultimately to be explained in terms of the real alienation or absenting of a more basic level of reality ingredient in it, its true essential nature or real (intrinsic) self. Alienation in thought – conceptual alienation – is thus to be explained in terms of the real alienation of human beings in their various social contexts and ultimately both are to be explained in terms of self-alienation, i.e. alienation from their true natures or intrinsic selves, from both their inner nature or soul or Self and their outer nature as (aspects of) Totality (or the cosmos) and from both as (part of) God. The fundamental cause of this may of course be conceptual – *avidya*, or ignorance, of our essential nature. How this *avidya* is to be understood and overcome will be discussed in the course of the narrative of the book.

This mode of false being is not (or not just) false as an account or in itself, but *false in virtue of being contrary to the true nature of human beings*. It thus depends upon the possibility of acting other than in accordance with the true nature of the self, i.e. upon *free will*, or upon the effects of such action objectified as social structures, in what has been called 'structural sin'.

This is paradigmatically, or at least depends upon,

α activity, life or being *contrary* to the true or fundamental, existentially constitutive (or ingredient), real intrinsic essential nature of the being (under the appropriate description) involved; but also encompasses,

β merely *incomplete* or unfulfilled, less than fully realised, being (whether in a single state, situation, mode of embodiment or timespan; or a series or succession of them).

The assumption behind (*β*) is that every being has a transfactually aefficacious and eventually realised conatus, urge or developmental tendency (for example, manifest in some learning process) to fulfil itself and express its true nature, that is, to flourish and realise its full potential, *ceteris paribus*: in, despite and through its being thwarted by contrary circumstances or constrained by countervailing forces, constituting or constituted by so many heteronomous orders of determination.[22]

speak, packed or inscribed within (or hovers over like a veil), forming an epi-structure to, the true nature of being. And it is this feature (stratification) which explains (2).

22 This concept of a tendency which is *eventually* realised is stronger than most of the concepts discussed in *DPF*, p. 78n. It could be dubbed a tendency e*. Its connection with desire, intentionality and thought generally will be discussed later.

If all relative being is characterised by development and change, and this depends upon a modicum of polarity and inner contradiction, it is not necessarily of type (α), which may be restricted to the human world analytically. Even if it is not, we may want to distinguish demi-relative reality from relative reality by the fact that division, absurdity and self-alienation all characterise non-human reality, if they can be said to characterise it at all, only as it were contingently; whereas in the human world they are all, directly or indirectly, manifestations of the *alienation of self-consciousness* (or of the Self in consciousness), i.e. of the alienation of what is a fundamental, essential and unique feature of human being. Demystification and self-consciousness[23] would thus seem to be essential to (the dialectic of) Self-realisation of human beings as such.

Notice that in both the cases of (2) and (3) the false constitution of being may persist, even if and when they are correctly described. Each of (1), (2) and (3) depends on a constitutive *absence*, that is, of a level of *structure* (or a degree of totality), which can then be shown by immanent–ideology–explanatory–critique (and/or by analogical-retroductive–hermeneutical–transcendental–dialectical argument) to explain the self-contradictory or absurd thought or practice; or to put it otherwise, upon a layer or realm of ingredient being, the real omission of which explains absurd and self-contradictory concepts and activities (both of which may, and indeed must, be analysed dispositionally), and the structures and relations which perpetuate them. In each case, real absence generates a potentially multiple series of levels of interlocking, or at least intersecting chains of *avidya–tina* formation: (emergent) heteronomous determination, chains which are ultimately grounded in the real alienation of man from God,[24] or so I shall urge.

Let me summarise. The aporiai, antinomies, dilemmas, dichotomies and paradoxes of contemporary thought are the aporiai of demi-reality, characterised by self-alienation and heteronomous orders of determination or constraint. They are ultimately to be explained in terms of the real (causally aefficacious)–irrealist (in character)–demi-real (false but dependent)–categorial structure of social reality, in which conceptual alienation is underpinned by real practical alienation, and

23 Rather than merely growth and development, in which sense it could be said entirely generally that error was a part of learning and that there could be no liberation save from constraint. However, transposed to the human context this truism generates the important theorems that there could be no enlightenment without *avidya* and that if we are already enlightened, no recognition or realisation of it without a prior forgetting (or fall), no unveiling without some (chronologically and/or analytically prior) veil. Moreover, this itself seems to be part of what is meant by the process of learning in the human world. Not just Self (which we already are) but consciousness of Self – or Self-consciousness – a Self-consciousness from which we are at present alienated.

24 And in particular from the real absenting of modes of presenting the transcendent – most characteristically through modalities of creative silence, or more generally absence – in dialectics of what I will call 'inaction'.

both by real alienation from our true nature or self; that is to say, they are ultimately to be explained by *deep rooted though objectively real philosophical mistakes*, mistakes which lie within the traditional province of causally aefficacious and causally explicable philosophy (as concerned with the categories).[25] This generates ontological insecurity and attachment, giving rise to fear, conflict and desire, and persists in virtue of a real absence, the absenting of the presence of the deep, ultimate, actual but occluded, categorial structure of the world: God, unity and love.

Philosophical irrealism is an ensemble or package which reflects, and in a sense correctly though only superficially and incompletely describes (and so cannot explain), a demi-world characterised by real irrealism, alienation and reified social forms (such as money), split, instrumental reasoning, conditionality, suffering, fear, division, oppression and multiple heteronomous orders of determination. Realist philosophy can play a diagnostic and corrective, politically transformative role here. In particular, the conceptuality of social life entails (through hermeneutics) a central role for transcendental arguments (from activities conceptualised in the experience of the agents concerned) and hence for dialectical arguments and thence for immanent–ideological–explanatory critiques. But the aefficacy of ideology–critique depends upon its capacity to (help) initiate or infuse a dialectic of self→Self-realisation turning upon transform*ed* transformative practice. Such practice will eventually take us all the way from the dialectic of desire to freedom, through the unity of theory and practice in absolute reason or cosmic consciousness, and through the shedding of the layers of structural illusion and heteronomous determination which veil or otherwise distort social reality to universal Self-realisation in the flourishing of each and all in 'unity existence', i.e. in universal Self-determination. The philosophy of critical realism thus passes over into the philosophy of universal Self-realisation, in which the alienation of human beings from their true intrinsic (both inner and outer) natures is transcended and heaven or eudaimonia is immanentised on earth. Where there was *maya*, there will be light.

1.4 For God

Realism about (α) *God* presupposes realism about (β) the *transcendent* (i.e. about transcendent beings) and that presupposes in turn realism about (γ) *transcendence* (the human capacity to transcend existing states or levels of consciousness, including knowledge). (β) is already a part of transcendental realism, being

25 Note that we are committed to a realism *about*, as well as *in*, *philosophy*, one which is of course implied by constellational, conceptual, categorial and agentive realism alike.

implied *inter alia* by the incomplete, unfinished and open character of science; and (γ) is implied *inter alia* by the *creativity* essential to the logic – or better, dialectic – of scientific discovery and development, but, as we shall see, is equally essential to all human being and agency generally. Before I discuss (β) and (γ), I want briefly to outline and comment upon – in twelve steps (what I shall call the 'Twelve Steps to Heaven') – the main features of (α), i.e. the realism about God expounded and developed here.

Twelve Steps to Heaven

1 *Ontological realism* about God (in the ID) is consistent with, and indeed entails, *experiential* (including *epistemic*) relativism (in the TD), including pluralism, fallibilism and diversity (see 1.1 above); that is, with the view that God:

a *manifests* him/her/itself; and/or
b is *accessible* in a variety of different ways,

for example, at different times, through different (such as religious) traditions, in different circumstances, to different people. It follows from this, as we shall see in more detail in step twelve, that God is *both absolute* (unbounded) and *relative*; that is, manifest (perhaps such as a 'personal lord' such as Krishna or Christ), and accessed in a particular, and to that extent relative, form.[26] It should also be reiterated that this epistemological relativism (which defines the degree of truth within transcendental idealism) is consistent with a moment of concretely singularised *judgemental rationality* (in the IA) in, say, the assessments of the claims of specific religious practices.

2 The experiential or *epistemic transcendence* of God is consistent with his *ontological immanence*, immanence within being, as indeed constellationally overreaching it (or rather the rest of being, the field of dependent being, of relativity, the created world or cosmos), defining its bounds.

But how is God immanent? God is immanent in (although perhaps to varying degrees) other parts of being as the ultimate but ingredient categorial structure of the world; as its most basic truth and ground (see the categorial realism developed in 1.3 above), on which the rest of being is unilaterally existentially dependent, but to which it is causally and taxonomically irreducible (see the

26 Thus even if it is experienced *as* absolute and the experience is of unboundedness, it is still *also* the experience of a bound physiology or whatever. We have to begin to think of God, superconsciousness, transcendental intuition, etc., in terms of categories such as constellational unity, including a moment of identity-in-difference, unity-in diversity and so on.

stratification of being discussed in 1.2 above). God, then, as the existentially constitutive ultimate (deepest, widest and most enduring) categorial structure of the world, including man, is thus *ingredient* in being. But God is neither

a *saturated* by, nor
b *exhaustive* of the rest of being (including man),

providing only the highest-order conditions of possibility of being or the rest of being, including those parts of being which obscure or otherwise work against him/her/it.[27]

From this, three corollaries follow:

3 (i) God, then, is ontologically ingredient in but not *saturated* by man (four-planar social being, nature, the cosmos). As ingredient in man, God is *ontologically immanent* – this is the God *within* (or inside) man, the 'inner God'. As unsaturated by man, God is ontologically transcendent – this is the God *without* – outwith (in Scottish) or outside – the 'outer God'. This defines an ontological *immanence/transcendence spectrum*, which may be discerned as postulates or presuppositions in particular (different) religious traditions or practices. The God inside and outside are ultimately to be unified.

(ii) As ontologically ingredient in, God is not *exhaustive* of (i.e. does not exhaust the being of) man or four-planar social being. The latter is rather overlain by levels of *maya* (illusion), which occlude, dislocate and distort it. This is 'structural sin', the result *inter alia* of man's free will. God affords or *enables*, man *selects*.

(iii) As the deep actual, though occluded and overlain, categorial structure of man is God, man is essentially God, already essentially free, even now already enlightened; an enlightenment, freedom and Godliness that has only (!) to be experientially accessed, stabilised in his consciousness and so realised in practice. God is actualised in man's essence but not in his consciousness (or self-consciousness), being, activity or life (although God is present, as a trace, condition and a potentiality in all of these). The ultimate nature of man is spirit (God-stuff, the substance of God), concretely singularised (individualised and to be individuated) as such. Souls are manifest or embodied as persons which come to Self- (and God-)consciousness over a succession of lives (spans or modes of embodiment).

4 God is both (i) *absolute* – independent (self-sufficient, autonomous) being, and (ii) *alethic* – the ultimate ground or deepest categorial truth of all other things,

27 God both contains and is beyond all genders; see 12 below.

and thence of all beings, i.e. *totality*. God is both the self-grounded ultimatum and the inner categorial core structure of reality; the existentially and essentially constitutive basic truth and ground of all grounds of the rest of it. God (α) *creates* (*β*), *contains* (bounds and binds, see step 9) and (γ) *categorially defines*, but does not exhaust, being. As self-sufficient, all-inclusive and deepest ground, constellationally overreaching the rest of being, God defines the conditions of possibility of all things, and hence all possibilities. Hence God is at once:

a *real*, as an absolute ground of pure dispositionality, the fount or field of all *possibilities*;

b *actualised*, as ingredient in man and (in various specific ways) the rest of being; and

c *experiencable* and *experienced* (in different ways, to varying degrees) in man – in human consciousness – and perhaps also (at least some of) the rest of being. God is real, as *absolute*, independently of the field of relativity, i.e. whether or not it is actualised (for instance, before creation); and actualised, in the domain of *relativity*, whether or not it is experienced (as such) in objectively constituted *demi-reality* (for example, before consciousness of enlightenment). $d_r \geq$(contains but is not exhausted by) $d_a \geq d_e$, and spirit–soul–person.

5 As unbounded (absolute) God, as we have just seen, (α) *creates* but also (*β*) bounds, i.e. is the unbounded boundary of (and binds (*β*', see step 9)), that is *contains* and unifies and (γ) *categorially defines* (providing the underlying perduring (γ') *continuant* informing or structuring) the rest of, i.e. relative (including demi-real), reality.

(α) corresponds to God as an *ultimatum*, in which creation must be *ex nihilo*. For were it not autopoetic, from nothing, from *absence*, from pure and simple – though perhaps infinite (unbounded) – unboundedness, the absolute would be limited, i.e. not unbounded, because bounded by something outside itself.[28]

(*β*) corresponds to the aspect of God as a *totality*, and (α) and (*β*) together constitute being as an open *absent totality*. As (α) unbounded (ontologically)

28 Creation is, epistemologically (transcendentally), *ex nihilo*; ontologically, from an unbounded, infinite, openness, which in turn may be given a cosmological declension of emptiness or the void – that is, the absolute as itself an *absent* (unbounded, limitless, supra-human-experiential, infinitely open and therefore transcendentally empty, but also full and beyond emptiness and fullness (plenitude)) *totality* – as various inflections on the absolute as an absent (open) totality.

and creative (epistemologically, axiologially), God is absent; as (*β*) bounding, a totality; as the constellational identity of both an (open) absent totality.

(γ) corresponds to the *universal ingredient* aspect of God, the sense in which it is said 'everything has a Buddha nature'. *Inter alia* this grounds

(δ) the essential unity of man as a particular species, and of all [human] modes of accessing God.

But God may, and arguably must, be ingredient in different species to differing degrees[29] and/or in different ways. So what are the *differentia specifica* of God's ingredience in man? Creation *ex nihilo* is implicit in every transformative act, which is always an emergence out of (from) absence, and is paradigmatically and ideally *spontaneous*, i.e. without mediation, conditionality (or instrumentalisation) or attachment (and therefore not karmically binding). Human creativity *ex nihilo*, ingredient in every genuine act, is thus in mimetic reproduction of and heterocosmic affinity with God's creation of the world.

6 God, as the source of everything, is also the (creative, absent) source of *creative intelligence*. But, as such, God's nature is obviously itself both creative and intelligent; that is, it includes – though as unbounded, it is not exhausted by or reducible to – these features.[30] And as such, God's nature also includes *consciousness* defined in the most minimal way, as the dispositional capacity to acquire or create and creatively manipulate or use (or creatively experience the effects of the use of) symbols and other media (including sound, light, *chi* and so on).[31] Furthermore, as such, God becomes potentially accessible to man *in* consciousness *as inter alia* consciousness; for example, in moments of transcendence, or more generally (exercises or experiences of) creative intelligence. So God is at least *also* consciousness.[32]

7 The proof of God's existence is experiential and practical. (And God, though

29 Some may, so to speak, contain more (or higher aspects of) God.

30 It may be thought to have been 'injudicious', but it was certainly an intelligent act to create and sustain – this is γ' God as, underlying, qua basic categorial structure, continuant – (other) intelligences, including intelligences which could come *inter alia* to recognize or remember God.

31 This way of defining consciousness allows us to sustain the idea that everything is or at least contains at least partially (even if only as the product of, or as conditioned or existentially/essentially constituted by) or potentially also is consciousness (for example, qua developing (enduring), in process); although man is perhaps uniquely conscious of his consciousness, and therefore possessor of potential degrees of self-consciousness, or consciousness of consciousness of self.

32 And since consciousness is irreducible to matter or, at least arguably, anything else limited in the way the relative field typically is, we could equally also say: consciousness is at least *also* (or partakes of) God.

enduring ingredient *essence* of, may be more or less (as well as differentially) experienced and/or realised by men).

8 God may be more or less realised by man; and man's intrinsic nature or *dharma* is to realise God both inner and outer, within and without. As the ultimate categorial structure of man (his real essence or true nature, overlain and occluded by other levels whose condition of possibility but not actuality it is), it manifests itself as an inner urge or developmental tendency to realise itself – through embodiment over a succession of lives – in two dimensions or orientations of self-expansion, corresponding to two aspects (inner and outer) of our intrinsic nature:

1 as an inner dialectic of self→Self-realisation, in the individual Self or soul; and
2 as an outer dialectic, oriented to universal Self-realisation, of self→Self (Totality)-realisation.

(2) manifests initially for all other individual selves in four-planar social being and then, in co-operation with (i.e. in virtue of the aefficacious grace of) God and other like-minded creatures (i.e. Godliness everywhere), for all beings and totalities in the cosmos as a whole, which, no less than man, have the right to fulfil themselves or become what they essentially are – Godlike or heavenly – so that the created world becomes (in, through and for itself) the material embodiment of God. For man, this involves freedom as autonomy or Self-determination, including liberation from (i.e. the disemergence of) heteronomous orders of determination.

9 This is to be aeffected by dialectics of de-alienation, including self-transcendence or Self-realisation, or re-union or practice(s) of yoga (or union) – of self with Self, of self with Totality and of self with God. On these dialectics, and their aspects and interconnections, I will have more to say anon. The important point to note here is that they all depend essentially upon (unconditional) *love*. Love expands, binds, unites and heals (making whole), and thus is crucial to yoga and de-alienation or re-union. God is *inter alia* but essentially love. As such, God is truly the cement of the universe, binding it together with the unifying power of love, in holistic and heterocosmic causality. The dialectics of de-alienation (of re-totalisation) are all essentially dialectics of love: of love of self (→Self), of each and all (→Totality) and, in both inner and outer movements, both as essentially love of God. The essence of liberated man is therefore love of God, and God, we could say, is not only essentially love but essentially to be loved.[33]

33 Fear, by contrast, is the polar opposite of love. Stemming from existential insecurity (produced by alien-

This, then is God as *unconditional* love, as the unifying, totalising, *liberating* power of the universe. Conversely attachment and aversion, and the conditionalities which characterise them, are at once tendentially auto-subversive and karmically binding.

10 We have, then, God as (deep, occluded but actual) enduring *ingredient essence*, but subject to greater or lesser degrees of *experience* by and of *realisation*, i.e. manifestation or embodiment in the relative, and especially the demi-real world of humanity. However, note that as God is the highest-order, enduring and existentially constitutive condition of its possibility, a perennially (or an enduring) fallen world, characterised by conceptual, real and self-alienation and the modalities of structural sin, is not possible; that is to say, it cannot be enduring and is not sustainable. So liberation, even though man may on the way destroy the *structures*[34] of other levels of being and the *conditions* of his forms of embodiment (such as on earth), is inevitable. (It is not *whether*, but *when* and with *how much* damage or harm to the rest of creation this occurs.) Moreover the dialectics of self-realisation and God-realisation, driven by the dialectic of desire for freedom (ultimately to freedom as self-determination), will always tendentially undermine a fallen world (as will the dialectics of individual and collective karmic learning processes or teaching situations). Thus, as the soul is immortal, realised enlightenment or being, Self-realisation, is inevitable. The conatus, tendency e*, to freedom must win out, though when, where and how are all contingent.

This is so not only for each individual soul, but equally for all souls and all species everywhere – truly universal enlightenment and flourishing, the immanentisation of heaven on earth – or, at least if not now on this planet, sometime, somewhere in the cosmos. This can be shown along both orientations of self-expansion, for each soul considered in itself as Self; and for each soul considered in solidarity and ultimately 'unity existence' with each other, which are equally its own conditions of being, and so therefore for each soul considered as Totality.

ation from self) and coupled to attachment (in the negative guise of aversion) fear contracts, divides, splits, alienates, ruptures, wounds. It tends, moreover, precisely through the creative power of thought, to produce exactly the situation feared, i.e. the state of which the agent is afraid, so that it is tendentially self-fulfilling. By the same token, intentional states of desire or wanting, expressing (positive) attachment – or (negatively) aversion to the situation in which they are expressed – tend to replicate that situation, i.e. the very situation in which the desire is expressed, as one of lack, so that they are equally and (paradoxically, for the very same reason) tendentially self-undermining. At the same time, the positive bi-polar of the negative state realised, the fear faced, the desire satisfied, sows the seed for future *karma*, attachment to attachment thus linking the evolving soul into the cycle of rebirth and redeath, until neither the desire for desire nor the fear of fear (nor *conditional* love, that is love that requires reciprocity) persists.

34 Structures in the (token as distinct from type) sense of *structurata*, to invoke Andrew Collier's useful concept. See *DPF*, p. 50 and *passim*; A. Collier, *Scientific Realism and Socialist Thought*, Hemel Hempstead, 1989.

11 The means to achieve these goals – of self-realisation for each and for all – depend upon absenting the present and presenting the absent in moments of transcendence, eventually to be stabilised in 'cosmic consciousness' or enlightenment, i.e. absenting the absence of the absence, namely the presence of God, both inner (as our higher selves) and outer, in our lives.

12 The fact that God or the absolute is unbounded does not mean that it cannot be experienced. It can be experienced *in* unbounded consciousness precisely as *unbounded* and furthermore experienced as unbounded beauty, love, power and so on. The experience is *of* a bound subjectivity (such as in some limited physiology), but *in* that experience the distinction between the (bound, relative) subject and its (unbound, absolute) object collapses, in a moment – characteristic of 'transcendence' – of subject–object identity, in which alterity, otherness – and with it the possibility of both referential detachment and emotional attachment – give way.

In such moments of identity – or what I shall call 'transcendental identity consciousness' (TIC) or 'superconsciousness' – the (ertswhile) subject is constellationally both united (at one) with and engulfed by the transcendent. And in such moments of 'transcendental intuition', more precisely of transcendental identification or union (yoga or de-alienation), of transcendental identity, which presupposes the constellational *non-identity* of the terms of the experience,[35] what is experienced is both God, the absolute, the unbounded, *and*, as the essential basis of that experience, the ingredient categorial structure or essential nature of man. One is thus experiencing at once both God within and God without. The same principle is true even if the God without is a manifestation in the relative field, for example a personal lord such as Krishna or Jesus.[36]

35 DCR does not deny that identity (here specifically subject–object identity) occurs in moments or states of transcendence but insists only that it presupposes the non-identity of the terms (which are at most constellationally identical) so that referential detachment (and hence the possibility of emotional attachment) is always possible.

36 Transcendence is not necessarily of (intuition of, or identification with) the absolute; what is transcendent can itself be in the relative field. So we must distinguish the *epistemically relative absolute* or ultimatum-for-us, both from (a) the absolute (and highest-order ingredient) and (b) its manifestation in the field of relativity, whether either or both are known as such to us (see 1.2 above). This is a distinct point from saying:

1 that the unbounded may be, and in principle must be, *itself unbounded*, i.e. infinite in terms of depth, extension and so on; and furthermore

2 that it may be, precisely as such, *gradable* (differentiatable, whether in human experience or not, and rankable) – in a manner akin to transfinite mathematics – in terms of degrees of depth, extension and so on of unboundedness;

3 that it, or some definite degree of it, may be itself dependent on a higher-order absolute or degree of unboundedness/infinity, so that it is only a 'relative' (or quasi-dependent) *absolute-in-itself*, whether we know it or not;

The fact that God is unbounded, and in principle consists (also) of infinite (layers of) depth and (zones or swathes of) extension does not mean that he can have no positive qualities (rather he has infinite qualities) or that he can only be defined by the *via negativa*, as not this, not that and so on. It does mean, however, that we must say that God is *both* consciousness, love, truth, bliss and so on, *and* beyond consciousness, love, truth, bliss and so on. Incidentally the relative absolute (absolute-for-us) may or may not be absolute-in-itself; and even if it is, it may be characterisable by different degrees of unboundedness, i.e. need not be simple or undifferentiated, as already noted in the footnote above.[37]

There are two final points to stress about TIC. The first concerns the *via negativa*. The fact that in the 'non-dual' state of TIC, alterity (otherness) and so on collapses, so that it cannot be *described* as such or in any other way *during* the state of TIC, does not mean that it and its properties cannot be described after, before or on the threshold (*ritambhara*) of the state. To suppose otherwise is precisely to commit a (displaced) variant of the epistemic fallacy, which would confound and identify being (here, the being of the state of consciousness) and its description. Second, this state, characterised by freedom from heteronomous determination, allows immediately a great negentropic influx of unbound and undissipated energy (that is, energy not required for use at other levels of activity and/or in sustaining or counteracting other levels of constraint) and, when stabilised 'in cosmic consciousness', in the activity of the agent, it issues in spontaneous right action, activity to maximum aefficacy and with least effort. That is to say, the non-dual experience of TIC is at once most energising and most energy-economising.

I have been discussing some properties of ontological realism (in the ID) about God under the general rubric of 'Twelve Steps to Heaven'. I now turn specifically to the experiential or quasi-epistemic question (in the TD) of means of accessing God.

What are the modes of accessing God? Let us consider this in three stages, moving through varieties of transcendence and of transcendent being to modes of

4 that (whether or not, but perhaps especially if (2) holds, so that it is differentiated, shaped or structured in terms of degrees of unboundedness) it may be such that it is *qualitatively describable* in itself by the use of terms originally or paradigmatically employed in the characterisation of attributes in the relative field (such as grace, love, compassion, beauty, power and so on). This last is a distinct point from saying

5 that we can validly *infer* properties of the absolute *from* (but not normally *during*) though we may perhaps be able to do so on the edge or *threshold* (*ritambhara*) of) TIC.

Both these last two points are however grounded in the same consideration, namely that the absolute, unboundedness and so on *also* exists in the relative field, as *ingredient* in man.

37 In fact it is probably better to conceive it (perhaps monadically or implicately (in Bohm's sense)) as all-pervasive rather than atomic; and even if it is simple, there may be boundless degrees (realms, orders) of simplicity, of the infinitesimal, of emptiness, zero or the void (absence or nothing).

accessing (experiencing) and realising God, including our God-nature, as agents eventually destined for a life of unconditional love. Before I do this, however, I want to consider some general properties of the concepts of (a) the *transcendent* and (b) *transcendence*.

Both (a) the transcendent and (b) transcendence are essentially relative concepts (that is, something is 'transcendent' relative to something else, or 'transcendence' occurs in respect of or in relation to a specific state), but both also have an absolute inflection or variant. Ontologically, the transcendent may mean something which is either (α) an outer *beyond* a given level (for example, of being, consciousness or experience) or (β) an inner *between* given levels (for example, of being, consciousness or experience – the space between as distinct from the space beyond), i.e. the gap, pause or hiatus. Developing (α) in its absolute inflection takes us to the concept of (α') the *unbounded*. This includes the idea of (α'') *emptiness* or *the void* or the vacuum state, that is the state of least excitation present in all other states, the sense in which the zero on a thermometer scale is present whatever the temperature, or the centre of a concentrically expanding circle is present whatever its expansion or the foundation of a pillar is present irrespective of its current height. (α') the unbounded is of course the absolute inflection of the transcendent. (α'') emptiness in the sense of the state of no – or at least, most minimal, simplest, purist form of – awareness takes us over to epistemological concepts of the transcendent. Thus here we have (γ) the transcendent as experientially (and more generally ontically) unmanifest, and derivative from this, (γ') the idea of the transcendent as epistemically unknown. This leads into two derivatives: (γ_1'), the idea of the transcendent as the source, such as the *nihilo* in creation *ex nihilo* (which may be just the gap between thoughts); and (γ_2'): the idea of the transcendent as the ultimatum, the envelope, the unbounded boundary of known or knowable being.

I move on now to (b) transcendence. The most basic concept here is perhaps that of overcoming some level of being, or consciousness or experience of being. Thus we have (α) the idea of transcendence in the sense of the sublating synthesis that overcomes dualism, contradiction and so on in the development of dialectical processes. But *within* this process (and achievement) of resolution, synthesis, sublation or transcendence (α), there is a moment of transcendence (β). This is the spontaneous moment or vanishing point of transcendence within the process of transcendence and prior to the transcending outcome – the state of co-presence or no-presence, the moment of creation *ex nihilo* when positive contraries are about to be transmuted into negative sub-contraries and both are, so to speak, instantaneously and simultaneously present (even if only coupled as traces) in the auric ambit of the conceptual field in question. (β) is also the moment of creation *ex nihilo*, from the gap, pause or silence (inspiration, rest or grace) or from the unbounded or the vacuum state or from the nowhere known. Finally (γ), we have transcendence in the sense in which I have been using it in 'transcendental identity consciousness', or TIC. And here it is worth stressing again that it is only *after* the non-dual experience and *in* the field of relativity that the experience (and properties of the state) can be defined or described. Second, we note again the energy influx that occurs with freedom from unnecessary forms of constraint or heteronomous determination. This sense of transcendence as TIC (γ) of course identifies transcendence with union with the unbounded or unboundedness itself; and thus by a short route with union with the Divine, and the process of immanentisation of transcendent being (or accessing the already (ontologically) immanent (epistemically) transcendent within us).

Transcendence is essential to scientific discovery and all human activity. Thus in the logic of scientific discovery there is, as we have just noted, a moment of transcendence within the process of transcendence, when a new transcending or sublating concept emerges (which is just another name for transcendence). Such a concept can be neither induced nor deduced from the existing field of data, but emerges 'out of the blue', from the space between or beyond, from nowhere, *ex nihilo* (out of nothing/non-being/absence (perhaps in moments of silence, play or rest, such as sleep)). Of course the ground for the creative discovery must be prepared. Thus it is typically from a transcendent cause on to an immanent ground, but creativity is essential to all human agency. Every human act is not only a transformation of what pre-existed it but also *de novo*, a novelty, a new beginning. In this sense it mirrors and mimics the creation. Emergence generally, as the bi-polar positive dual or correlative of absence, has the same logical form as the transcendence involved in human creativity but does not essentially involve consciousness, or at least self-consciousness, in the way the latter does.

Transcendence, in the sense of the move from a normal waking state of consciousness to a transcendental state or level (of superconsciousness), is an aim in meditation (namely union with the absolute) and can be characteristic of prayer, moments of silence or grace, a feature of many religious practices (in acts of worship or the experiencing or celebration of the sacred or the blessed). It is a feature of bliss experience, and may be experienced while listening to music, going for a walk, just being in nature and, for example, looking at the sky (the clouds, the stars at night), while surfing, and so on. It typically involves a feeling of *identification* (TIC) with a being, consciousness or experience beyond the normal and which is constituted by and/or emanating from a level of being (characteristically the source of the feeling) which engulfs or delights one. It abolishes, vanishes otherness in a moment of identity-in-difference with that which it identifies. Transcendence is alive, as experience, and present everywhere: its absence is most marked in irrealist philosophy and the alienations, reifications, dualisms and fragmentations which it at once undergirds and is proximately explained by.

This leads me on to the varieties of transcendent beings, here in the sense of beings epistemically (though not necessarily ontologically[38]) transcendent to one's current experience. There is God as absolute, alethic, independent being; deities and avatars (manifestations and embodiments of God); and angels (aspects of God or the divine will). Then there are aspects of the stratification of *our* being (such as our souls) not readily accessible to us. Then there are or may be subjects at very different levels of being; for example, there arise the possibilities of spirits at levels beyond embodiment but not manifest, or of, more subtle levels of embodiment, the denizens of the astral and causal worlds, including discarnate souls. Then there are, or may be, beings which exist and act at levels of vibration, including physical vibration, which render them not (currently or ever) accessible by or to human sense organs either (a) unaided, (b) aided prosthetically, (c) developed clairvoyantly, a possibility implicit in the unfinished, open-ended evolution of our species, which encompasses the possibilities of the further development[39] of our perceptual and moral (as well as our cognitive and technological) powers, (d) more generally developed by intuition, telepathy, the growth of paranormal or (otherwise put) the possibile liberation of perhaps normal psychic powers, or (e) developed through heterocosmic affinity and so on. This is to leave aside the possibilities opened by the notion of parallel and multiple universes, or of an infinite and unbounded extension (plurality) of universes, whether connected in some mode or not.

Accessing God may be as either outer or inner. As a transcendent outer in religious practices or as a transcendental inner in meditation, it typically occurs by abstaining from doing in order to be (to become more fully Self, for example, by excluding all but some real but higher state of being or consciousness), which can then ultimately be stabilised in all manner of activity in the relative world. This may be part of a deliberate practice of accessing the absolute in one form or another. But one may be at one with the absolute; or aware only of its presence; or of the aeffects of its presence; or of the aeffects of worship (for example, of the presence of the absolute) or of the aeffects of other religious practices. The presence of God may manifest itself in the absent silence of consciousness or in activity, just as God may appear or manifest or realise or present itself in many different media, modes of embodiment or incarnations or more generally forms and ways. To access God and make him one with the Self is to find one's true identity in Self or soul (and in thence spirit as Self or Totality in 'unity consciousness'). One is then both fully an individual and fully God (Godlike) and full of God, fully oneself as Self and fully (and perhaps for the first time) free.

38 The God within him or herSelf.

39 Or rather (perhaps) their fuller actualisation in the context of our self-developmental or learning (karmic) evolutionary processes.

Summary of 1M

In the introduction to the book, I established that the aporiai in contemporary thought stem from real alienation and absence, and ultimately from the alienation of man from himself and God; that is, and above all, the root of the problems that beset our social thought and contemporary society itself lie in terms of self-alienation. *The* fundamental malaise then is self-alienation, and this underpins a chain of *avidya–maya* dualism, multiple and heteronomous orders of determination and degrees of constraint (ultimately grounded in man's free will, including free will objectified collectively and structurally as 'structural sin')–alienation–reification–conditionality–attachment–ontological insecurity–fear (stemming from self-alienation)–*tina* formation–denegation–reflexive inconsistency (lack of unity of theory and practice in practice, stemming from non-self-consciousness of man's enlightenment).

Section 1 – and by far the longest part[40] – of the present general theoretical introduction has dealt with 1M, or ontology. In the first sub-section on ontology I considered the arguments for ontology and established the necessity of it as a subject, and also its general shape or content. Everything is contained within being; to alienate anything is to dualistically split being and make one or other part of being (and ultimately both) causally inexplicable or inaefficacious.

Sub-section 1.2 treated of dispositional realism. In it I considered the stratification of being, including the topics of emergence and disemergence. These make free will, structural sin, heteronomous orders of determination, illusion and ideology possible but also make possible reincarnation, *karma* and *moksha* or liberation. Alongside and overlaying the co-presence of autonomous and various layers of heteronomous orders of determination is the co-presence of absolute, relative and demi-real being. Objectively constituted was differentiated from purely subjective illusion. Considering the topic of degrees or orders of (heteronomous) determination and constraint, this includes and may be theoretically embellished and glossed as ideology/illusion, impurity, *karma* (the presence of the past), attachment, supplementary or extraneous determination, heteronomy (as such), ingrained counter-conative habit or disposition based on (practical) *avidya*, excess baggage, and so on. Heteronomy is always manifest in attachment, set by *karma* and grounded in self-alienation, based on practical ignorance or *avidya* (especially of our true selves). These form a vicious interlocking circle. To break free from it is to become what we most truly are; this is our birthright and our task, our bounden duty and our joy: liberation.

40 Most that is pertinent in 2E–4D will be treated in depth in the narrative of the book, which however presupposes the ontology, and in particular the dispositional realism, categorial realism and realism about God and transcendence developed in Section 1.

A simple model sees three levels of action, the highest-order level consisting of grace, the second highest-order level consisting of *dharma* or action in accordance with the intrinsic nature of the particular concretely singularised human being, and the lowest order constituting various levels or degrees of heteronomous determination and constraint being constituted by *karma*. These are the three levels of action. There are differential responses to *karma*. These include first, transcending it, acting from the standpoint of the absolute or the unbounded or the gap; second, learning from it, a progressive response to *karma*; and third, satisfying and discharging it, letting go of it. The fourth all too familiar response is to remain encumbered by it, repeating over and over again the habitual reaction to the karmic situation or context. The three forms of action are: (1) spontaneous or carefree action; (2) careful or mindful focused action; and (3) attached or care-less action. Among the ultimata are two especially important continuants, the soul as the continuant of the self and God as the continuant of the universe. As ultimata, these are characterised by the dispositional identity of the thing and its powers. Therefore, it is not necessary to think of the soul as occurrent, rather than (merely) a disposition to be embodied or disembodied. This overcomes non-realist Buddhist objections to the idea of the immortality, and (one could say) the actuality, of the soul. Heteronomous orders of constraint, including ideology as lived illusion, consist in belief/want cognitively informed (belief-based) emotional complexes; and they too must be analysed dispositionally, namely as ingrained habitual dispositions. Fears and desires, and the beliefs that ground them, are all dispositions to behave in certain ways, which are only actualised when the appropriate situations materialise. This is how they can be carried on and discharged in the future, including, if unrealised in this life, in future lives. What binds individuals to the cycle of rebirth is the continued presence of ingrained habitual dispositions (grounded in some or other fear or desire based on attachment) to act in certain ways; and what liberates man from this cycle is the cessation of the intentional state of attachment. 'Let go and let God' is the appropriate emotional response to this situation. This is the same as *yagya* or surrender or sacrifice to the Lord. That is, in the terms of the *Bhagavad Gita*, the dedication of one's life to Krishna, but also of course equally to the Christ, Buddha or Allah or whoever. Understanding this fully (which is also acting on and implementing it) is a practical matter, as will be shown in the narrative of the book.

In sub-section 1.3, I argued for categorial realism. Categories are objectively real in the intransitive dimension, not subjective or transitive dimensional interpretations of reality. So we have the possibilities of, on the one hand, ignorance of ultimata or deep levels of structure and, on the other hand, that of the false categorisation of social being in the transitive dimension so as to speak quite independently of (or rather in the absence of) its real or true categorisation. Combining the insights of categorial and dispositional realism, we have the possibility that the alienation of a being at a level of reality is to be explained in terms of alienation from its intrinsic nature. In general terms, I argued that conceptual is to be explained in terms of real alienation, which is to be explained in terms of self-alienation, and that concepts of self, consciousness of the self and the nature of the self must all be conceived as developing (in differentiated ways).

In sub-section 1.4 on God, we considered twelve aspects of God's existence under the rubric of the 'Twelve Steps to Heaven'. Some of these corresponded to different moments of the stratification of being in 1M; others corresponded to aspects of 2E such as creativity and transcendence and emergence, all positive duals of absence; others corresponded to moments of the realm of totality in 3L; while still others corresponded to the dialectics of Self-realisation and God-realisation in 4D, so in a sense I could have written the whole of the general theoretical introduction under the rubric of this sub-section.

Turning to the topic of the transcendent, I distinguished the concepts of the beyond from the unbounded and both from that of the between, the gap, the pause or the hiatus. A variant on the unbounded consisted of emptiness or the void, and this took us into the topic of the vacuum state, a form of which is the state of least or simplest or perhaps no awareness, the non-dual state of transcendental consciousness. Other concepts of the transcendent included the experientially unmanifest and the epistemically unknown, including the idea of the ultimatum as the source and the boundary of all being. Moving on to the topic of transcendence (which, like the concept of the transcendent, is an intrinsically relative one though, like the former, with its absolute inflection), we differentiated transcendence as synthesis, resolution, reconciliation of opposites overcoming dualism, contradictions and so on – what I have called the τ moment in dialectical and developmental learning processes[41] – from the moment, within this moment of synthesis, of the emergence of the new concept. For within this moment of synthesis or sublation, there is a moment of transcendence within the transcendence. This is the transition point, at which the dialectics of co-presence in the form of the co-presence of positive contraries and negative sub-contraries is most apparent. This is the moment of creation *ex nihilo* from the gap, the unbounded or the vacuum state. In relation to the topic of transcendental identity consciousness, we noted that it is only after the non-dual experience and in the field of relativity that this experience and the properties to which it affords us access can be defined and described. We also noted the link between the negentropic energy influx which this experience endows us with and the freedom which it helps to afford from entropic heteronomous forms of constraint and degrees of determination. This is the excess baggage of human life which drains and interferes with

41 See *DPF* C1.6, p. 22.

that spontaneous right action that would otherwise flow intrinsically from being at one with our *dharma* or intrinsic nature. Identity consciousness may be paradigmatically attained at the level of transcendental consciousness or super-consciousness, where transcendental identification is obtained with the absolute or unbounded, but it should be noted that identity consciousness is also possible with non-absolute, relative beings, phenomena and so on.

In all this, consciousness is conceived in the first instance as a sort of cursor travelling up and down, accessing different states and levels of consciousness. From this point of view, states and levels of consciousness may also be conceived as part of the intransitive furniture of the world, as existing (at least dispositionally) independently of the 'self-consciousness' which will access them in a dualistic or non-dualistic way. In transcending heteronomous orders of determination, we must distinguish the case where the higher-order level provides sufficient conditions which lower-order heteronomous levels contravene, in which we are concerned essentially with a dialectic of purification and shedding, from the case where higher-order levels provide only necessary conditions with sufficient conditions subject to free will, a free will which may be exercised in accordance with those higher-order conditions as well as in contravention of it. Here we must be concerned with a dialectic of embodiment or realisation as well as of clearing or release; that is, of de-alienation, including integration and embodiment at all levels of being.

2 2E: Absence

In *DPF*, I argued that absence was a transcendentally necessary feature of being and that the omission of the concept of absence, the absence of absence, was the fundamental category mistake of Western philosophy from the time of Parmenides on. Absence, then, is necessary for presence, for any positive being at all. In particular, absence is necessary for process and change and vital to the topic of dialectic. It should be noted that there are two inflections or definitions of dialectic. On the first, dialectic is the absenting of absences or constraints on absenting absences or ills. On the second, it is the process or the experience of the process of the formation or dissolution of stratified and differentiated totalities. These 'negative' and 'positive' inflections amount to the same thing. In the architectonic of dialectical critical realism, 1M is a special case of 3L and 4D of 2E (depth is a special case of totality and action of negation). In *DPF*, various concepts of real negation including transformative or developmental negation and radical or self or subject negation were developed. Here I want to modulate my remarks around the critique of Hegelian dialectic.

It is convenient to divide critical discussion of Hegelian dialectic into four aspects. Its rational kernel, which is essentially a developmental or learning process, may be linked to the triad of ideas of reincarnation, *karma* and *moksha*. Its mystical shell is above all ontological monovalence or the absenting of the concept (and to an extent the reality) of absence in the irrealist categorial structures of contemporary society. Its golden nugget is the dialectics of co-presence including the dialectics of co-presence involved in moments of transition (that is, the coupling of positive contraries and negative sub-contraries) at the point (or junction) of the emergence of a new concept and the co-presence of modes of absolute, relative and demi-real being, together with that of the co-presence of necessary (such as realist) and false (such as irrealist) categorial structures in *tina* compromise formations and that of the connected co-presence of autonomous and (various degrees or levels of) heteronomous orders of determination in social life and human action. Finally, there is the platinum plate which is its diagnostic value in revealing the categorial structures of the societies in which the philosophical dialectic emerges and which it in a measure reflects. Before I come on to this, however, I want to say something about the characteristic normative duality of absence.

Absence has both a process, product or outcome and a normative duality. Normatively, negatively, incompleteness or lack generates contradiction, inconsistency, split, dualism or alienation. Positively, absence appears in the guise of the space (the gap or the unbounded) out of which there emerges the moment of transcendence and within this moment that moment of creativity, of generation *ex nihilo* in which I have argued every genuine human transformative act is in heterocosmic affinity with God's creation of the universe.

The basic structure of the Hegelian dialectic revealing its rational kernel as a general development process can be defined as follows:

> Absence (– error) – incompleteness – inconsistency (contradiction, etc.) – transcendence > to a greater totality

The dialectic here is initiated, powered, evidenced and remedied by absence.[42] Several features of this schema should be noticed. First, the absence–*tina* formation–heteronomous determination (via attachment and self-alienation) chain itself initiates the dialectic of desire for freedom. This has two declensions, the first to self-realisation and the second to universal self-realisation. This latter, 'unity existence', is one of the inflections of the term 'God-realisation'. Realised beings in turn may be divided into those creating no new *karma* but still subject to past

42 Understanding this schema in its totality shows that the normative negativity of incompleteness itself plays a positive role, so that it is itself (dialectically) part of the normatively positive duality of absence.

karma and those not creating new *karma* and free from (i.e. not subject to) past *karma*. Such beings are God or manifestations of God, or become Gods in their own right. This is the second inflection of the term 'God-realisation'. The dialectic of the desire for freedom therefore itself initiates by, it will be seen, a further twist of the inexorable logic of dialectic universalisability, freedom without desire and ultimately a world of freedom or autonomous self-determining individuals, who are realised beings, existing in unity existence, i.e. a realised community, at one with themselves and each other and indeed the totality, that is a world without desire or attachment.[43]

The second feature of this dialectic to note is that error, though it is not the same as, always depends on absence, that is an incompleteness of some kind. The error may take the form of *avidya*, that is to say deep-rooted categorial ignorance or mistake (including forgetting), an ignorance characteristic of the world of *maya* or demi-reality, of false being or illusion, of ideology as lived illusion (where the illusion is lived as an ingrained habitual disposition or dispositional complex). Behaviour in this world of lived illusion is, as we have seen, to be explained in terms of the real alienation, reification and so on characteristic of the irrealist categorial structure which informs the surface (and deeper, though not deepest) structures of society, and both of these are ultimately to be explained in terms of the real alienation of man from his true nature and the cosmos, a deep real absence.

Incompleteness of this (as indeed any) sort leads to split, dualism and alienation. Characteristic responses to it were mapped by Hegel in his figures of the beautiful soul, the stoic, the sceptic and the unhappy consciousness. The beautiful soul is isolated from his community. Pure unto himself, he is alienated from the society and world he must inhabit and upon which he ultimately depends. The stoic is indifferent to the incomplete world, the world of relative reality in which

43 This proceeds as follows: in desire we are committed to the removal of constraints on desires; and thence by the logic of dialectical universalisability to the removal of all dialectically similar constraints; and thence to the removal of all constraints as such in virtue of their dialectical similarity as constraints; and thence to the removal of the cause of all constraints (ills or suffering) – in attachment as such; and thence to the removal of its cause – *avidya* or lack of self-realisation (cosmic consciousness or enlightenment, i.e. the stabilisation of the absolute in the relative, the end to self-alienation, i.e. the expansion of self→Self-consciousness, that is the replacement of the empirical ego by the transcendental self through dialectics of inaction (and action) in the relative phase of existence). (The removal of this most fundamental form of *avidya* or ignorance is effected by the act of self-realisation, and its universalisation.) The true foundation of the eudaimonistic society as described in *DPF* is thus 'unity existence' as elaborated here. What makes a eudaimonistic society impossible without unity existence is the falsely or badly infinite (in Hegelian terms) character of desire, greed or craving (and the other negative emotional states which they imply, such as fear), which make them intrinsically repetitive and so unsatisfiable as such (that is as a state of desiring or whatever). In unity existence there is intentionality and achievement, but without desire and attachment to results or consequences.

he must also dwell. He is thus again split. The sceptic denies this alienated relative reality in theory but affirms it in practice and so is guilty of reflexive or performative contradiction. The unhappy consciousness holds both aspects of the contradiction in his consciousness, which is divided between the this-worldly immanent relative world and the other-worldly transcendent absolute world, a split he cannot reconcile.

The resolution of this sequence of contradictory attitudes to self alienation or indeed incompleteness of any fundamental type is transcendence to a new higher phase of consciousness and being, which must ultimately be cosmic consciousness or enlightenment. Only a consciousness which stabilises the absolute in the relative will be free of the alienations and illusions of demi-reality. Besides (or as forms of) split, incompleteness generates dualism, alienation, fragmentation, inconsistency or contradiction, anomalies, aporiai and other crises and ills. These constitute its characteristic epistemic symptom and act as a signal for a move to a more transcendent, totalising, concept or way of being which will remedy the incompleteness and thence reconcile the inconsistencies in a greater, richer, fuller or deeper totality. If what is omitted is axiologically necessary, then we have that form of co-presence which is *tina* formation.

Transcendence depends upon, as we have already seen, creativity; and emergence just is the positive bi-polar dual of absence. Creativity is implicit in all agency. It is, as I have already stressed, a form of (normatively positive) absence, of becoming *ex nihilo* and it constitutes, as already stressed, the transcendental element within the moment of transcendence. The dialectic which stems from self-alienation ultimately leads to greater self-realisation and issues in spontaneous right action. This is maximally coherent and equally least effort action. From this standpoint, there is a greater amount of energy more economically and efficiently used. The action occurs, as it were, from a deeper and wider standpoint, from the standpoint of a totality greater than the individual empirical ego and so commands what can be called 'nature-support'. De-alienation generally depends on yoga or reunion at all four planes of social being under the dominance of (d),[44] that is, the dialectic of self to Self, in the stratification of the personality. But that must proceed too, as we shall see later,[45] in a dialectic of collective and totalising agency as well. These correspond respectively to the moves to transcendental and God-consciousness, ultimately to be unified in the development of unity

44 See *DPF C9*, p. 160, *PE CS–SRHE* C2 *passim* for discussion of the 'social cube' in four-planar social space, defined by the co-ordinates of (a) material transactions with nature, (b) transactions between persons, (c) social structures and (d) the stratification of the personality. This conception needs to be further refined to allow for the possibility of non-physical levels of embodiment and subtle (not physically manifest or obvious) levels of interaction, and more generally causality, effect and being.

45 See especially Chapters 6 and 7 below.

consciousness. Reverting for a moment to the topic of the (Hegelian) unhappy consciousness, let me just remark that it is an aim of this book to help to reconcile the contemporary unhappy consciousness of the planet, split between the other-worldly transcendental impulses of the East and the this-wordly immanent relative emphases of the West. At the highest level, these two impulses take us on a conatus to cosmic and God-consciousness respectively, and they are to be reconciled in unity consciousness and ultimately in the being of unity existence. This, then, is the rational kernel of the dialectic as an epistemological, more generally developmental learning process, turning on absence in all its aspects. It immediately leads on to the topics of reincarnation, *karma* and *moksha* or liberation. But before I discuss these, let me deal more briefly with the other three aspects of the critical reception of Hegelian dialectic, namely the mystical shell, the golden nugget and the platinum plate.

The mystical shell is, as we have seen, above all Hegel's ontological monovalence, which results in his fixism and endism. But it is also overlain by Hegel's philosophy of identity. Against this, DCR affirms the dialectic of dialectical and analytical reasoning. A centre point of this is a critique of the fixity of the subject in the subject/predicate form. A crucial concept here is that of subject negation, that is the negation, transcendence or transformation, not only of ideas about the subject including the self, philosophy, God, identity, object, objectivity and so on, but also the negation or development of those subjects, selves, objects and so on themselves.[46] This takes us of course immediately into the theme of the dialectic of self-realisation – and ultimately of God-realisation in unity existence, that is, generalised embodied heaven on earth – but the topic of subject negation also embraces the characteristic method of philosophy. This is, on the conception which I have developed in *DPF* and elsewhere as generalised phenomenology, essentially immanent critique. Dialectical is to be conceived as continuous with transcendental argumentation and both with retroductive analogical explanation in scientific and ordinary life. For its part, the critique of the notion of the object leads to critique of atomistic and punctualist conceptions of the self and subjectivity. We have already noted some implications of the critique of an individual thing and an event, namely in biology and in quantum physics respectively. For instance in biology, we have the notion of an individual, or more properly a species, in its environment (*Umwelt*) replacing the idea of an isolated organism. In quantum physics, we have the idea of an event as a collectivity or totality, a distribution (or in my terms) a rhythmic in space–time, a most useful model for

46 Insofar as the source (or causes) of the subject's negation is entirely endogenous, i.e. it is self-generated, subject negation is equivalent to what I called in *DPF* (C1.3 and C2 *passim*) 'radical negation'. Radical negation is the prior, and ultimately determining, moment in all dialectics of self-realisation, whether of action or inaction, as we shall see below.

explicating the *karma* of an event, situation or relationship. In sociology, we have the idea of four-planar social being incorporating the idea of the unfinished and developing evolution of the species including its moral, cognitive and perceptual powers. To these four planes we must add in principle the possibility of multi-dimensional relational and further energetic levels of being. Corresponding to the critique of subjectivity, we have the critique of abstract and reified conceptions of objectivity, critiques then of atomism and closure.

Moving on to the dialectics of co-presence, we have already noticed four instances of this: the co-presence or coupling of positive contraries and negative sub-contraries in moments of transition in the emergence of new concepts or levels of being; the co-presence of levels of absolute, relative and demi-real being; the co-presence of necessary and false conceptualisations in *tina* formations and the co-presence of autonomous and heteronomous orders of determination. The co-presence of realist and irrealist categorial structures corresponds respectively of course to those of autonomous and heteronomous orders of determination. It is the co-presence of the real and the irreal (the demi-real) in stratified shifting *tina* formations which will play such a central role in the dialectic of what I will call 'shedding', that is, of heteronomous determinations, or more properly the dialectic of the co-presence of (and struggle between) pre-existing but unrealised autonomous and emergent but unnecessary heteronomous determinations.

I turn now to the platinum plate, in which philosophy is used as a diagnostic clue to the character of social or more generally human reality. The first level of effect is the deprocessualisation consequent upon the irrealist ensemble or package defined by ontological monovalence and characterised by real alienation, ontological insecurity and fear, leading to attachment and desire, which will ultimately undermine itself in the dialectic of desire to freedom, that is to say, in a dialectic of self-realisation. The second level is dualism with its hidden aporiai, consequent upon the real alienation, reification, ontological monovalence and so on of demi-reality. At the third and deepest level, this real irrealist categorial structure, including the totality of characteristic split and combined *tina* formations, and the variety of heteronomous forms of determination, rests as we have seen ultimately on the self-alienation of man from himself, God and the cosmic totality of which he is an aspect. In this way it reveals the basic contradiction between real and irreal categorial structures, and autonomous and heteronomous orders of determination, reflecting the split between Self and self, that is the self-alienation of man or man's alienation of himself from his Self, and from God, totality and the cosmos.

Before I go on to discuss the transcendental deduction of reincarnation, *karma* and *moksha* or liberation, the dialectic in *From East to West*, and say a bit more about the dialectical critique of analytical reasoning, I want to focus on a 4D counterpart of absence: inaction. The modalities of inaction include (1) abstaining from action, either (a) in the sense of failure to act (whether deliberate or not, and whether well motivated or otherwise) or (b) in the sense of the suspension (usually deliberate) of action, for example in processes of meditation or self-transcendence; (2) spontaneous or basic unmediated effortless action – this is inaction as spontaneous right action;(3) minimum action; (4) creation (production *ex nihilo*, from the gap or the unbounded); (5) action by implosion, collapse or more generally transformation into an opposite; (6) action with minimum force, leading to no force; (7) defencelessness or *ahimsa*, the path of no resistance; and (8) unconditional love, that is, selfless (with a small) action. The relation between these modalities of inaction will be explored in the narrative of the book.

Deduction of the necessity for reincarnation turns essentially on three features: first, that of universal causality; second, that of the emergence, i.e. causal and taxonomic irreducibility, of intentional states to the physical states through which they are manifest; and third, following on from the first and second, (a) the causal explicability of intentional phenomena, presupposing the pre-existence and (b) the causal aefficacy of intentional states implying the post-existence of the being who is the subject of the intentional state. The continuant in question is customarily called the soul. However, as already indicated, the soul need not be conceived as an occurrent thing. Rather it may be thought, as a relative ultimatum, as a disposition (dispositionally identical with itself), as indeed are the intentional cognitive/emotional states which, when states of attachment, drive the dialectic of reincarnation on. *Moksha* depends upon the cessation of the intentional state of attachment, reincarnation occurs because of it and *karma* occurs in virtue of it. Thus we only get just what we choose,[47] or rather what we get is just an aspect of what we do. *Karma* – action – has aspects which spread out into the past and into the future. The possibility of giving irreducibly psychological or socio-psychological explanations of intentional phenomena presupposes the pre-existence of the soul prior to the physical embodiment to or in which the phenomena occur. Similarly, the irreducible causal aefficacy of ideas, and intentional states generally, presupposes the post-existence of the souls involved in them. Without the supposition of reincarnation there are insufficient causes and insufficient consequences of intentional states and actions for the thesis of ubiquity determinism, that is insufficient explanations and aeffects for differences in the human social world.

To deny reincarnation or *karma* involves a dualistic split between agency or action and agent. This is a residue of reason/cause, mind/body dualism. We either have to deny that reasons have and/or produce causes and consequences, or that

47 For example, some situation we need to complete our experience of, a desire we wish to see realised, an intention or project which we need to fulfill, etc.

they are in the same world as those causes and consequences. To suppose that they are in the same world as those causes is to suppose that human existence predates and postdates the course or duration of a particular life.[48] The precise character and phenomenology of the intervals between lives need not concern us here, since the underlying continuant, namely the soul, has been defined dispositionally.

Karma is just the operation of this universal causality so construed as to allow for the ubiquitous irreducible causal explicacy and aefficacy of ideas and intentional states generally. It is indeed the only position consistent with what I have elsewhere called a synchronic emergent powers materialism. Often glossed in terms of concepts such as dependent origination and combined co-production, *karma* has a quantum-like holistic character in which the causes and effects of an action may be spread over many lives, situations and agencies. *Karma* may be collective as well as individual and may be displaced as well as transcended. The transcending agency may be the Self or the grace of some more transcending realised being. However the *karma*, if negative, will be merely mitigated or diminished; while if positive it may be amplified. Liberation occurs in two stages. First, no new *karma* is created. This occurs with the cessation or transcendence of the intentional state of attachment. Second, the individual is no longer subject to past *karma*. He is then free from the necessity to engage in the cycle of rebirth, redeath and reincarnation. He may however choose to do so if he assumes the mantle of a Bodhisattva, that is, one who is completely oriented to universal self-realisation. The real theme of this book is the operation of reincarnation, *karma* and liberation, so I will say no further about these topics here. They will be shown at work in detail in the narrative of the book.

The dialectic of *From East to West* operates at at least two levels. It is on the one hand a dialectic of the odyssey of a soul through a succession of lives driven (a) substantially, by desire or its perspectival equivalent fear (that is, lack in some intentional form), and (b) formally, by incompleteness. But it is secondly a dialectic of philosophical systems or world views. At this level it is also driven by incompleteness or lack, again as experienced by the soul or souls concerned. Thus in life nine the Chinese Taoist poet/priest, in what has been called 'the middle truth', wants to see emptiness or the void (the absolute) immediately manifest in nature and the phenomena of the ordinary material world, without for instance, social mediation, that is, any Confucian 'state mandate of heaven' or otherwise. One effect of this vision is an enlightenment in isolation and social alienation. This in turn sets the soul on a path which will lead him from individual liberation to compassion, and thence in life eleven to the formulation of the project of

48 It is important to note that if we deny reincarnation or *karma* then we once more dualistically split the world in two and initiate a characteristic chain of *avidya–tina* formation.

universal self-realisation. This in turn will necessitate the experiences of the path of action and the way of the householder rather than (or at least in addition to those of) the path of renunciation and the way of the recluse, which will take the soul into the socio-economic adventures of lives 12–15. In the dialectical philosophy, each system or position in turn can be seen to contribute something but in its turn omit something else, and the story must continue until the truth as whole is completed, and so the whole truth (or our best current approximation to it) can be told.

I turn finally in this section to the dialectical critique of analytical reasoning. We have already noticed the importance of the concepts of subject, self and radical negation. Ultimately all change in the social world depends on self-expansion leading to self-transcendence, that is, depends upon, even if it does not entirely consist in, radical negation, which is pivotal here for the concepts of subjecthood and selfhood. Subjects/selves are not fixed, let alone atomistic or punctual; rather they are stratified, rhythmically developing and particularised – concretely singularised – individuals. In a theoretical sequel to this work, I will have much more to say about the further dialectical development of the concepts of subject, self, thing, event, object, objectivity and so on.

3 3L: Totality

The dialectical critique of purely analytical reason (and the notions of subjectivity and objectivity which the latter imply) leads naturally into the subject matter of section 3, the realm of 3L or Totality, internal relationality and holistic causality. For the basic problem with analytical reasoning is that it implies that things are fixed and abstractable from their environment. On the contrary, the dialectical position sees things as being existentially constituted by their rhythmics or geo-histories and by the totality of their relations with other things. This naturally leads into a radical account of the self. What is normally understood by the self is an illicit abstraction from a much deeper and broader (and developing) totality. The stratified, rhythmically developing, concretely singularised – and vastly expanded – concept of the self leads naturally in its turn on to the topic of section 4, treating the 4D domain of transformative praxis. For while dispositional realism insists that it is a fundamental mistake to identify or reduce the nature of the self to agency (the fundamental theme of the *Bhagavad Gita*), it is nevertheless the case (and equally central to the *Gita*) that action from the standpoint of the Self is dharmic, spontaneously right and most creative, compassionate and coherent. This is the action of en-lightened man[49] and in section 4, and to a much

49 En-lightened man is not only illuminated (and illuminating), but less weighty (therefore lighter), having shed his illusions, layers of heteronomous determinations.

greater extent in the narrative of the book, we will go into the dynamics of his liberation.

Among the topics discussed in *From East to West* and/or its sequel (*Transcendence and Totality*) which fall under the rubric of 3L or totality are those of the self, comparative religion, East–West relations and philosophical ideologies. In the theoretical sequel to this book, I will treat at length such key notions as the concept of totality, alterity, things, events, subjects, objects, subjectivity, objectivity, abstraction, concretion, universality, singularity, internal relationality, duality verses dualism, holistic and heterocosmic causality, and the possibilities and opportunities raised by the unfinished evolution of the species. In this book, I will say something about the social cube, generalised concepts of body and alienation, dialectics of love, in particular of unconditional love and self-expansion, versus fear and desire, all of which turn on considerations relating to the grounding of the 4D concept of agency in the 3L concept of the self. In particular, I will consider the self-fulfilling or undermining, and carrying on or insistent, character of desire and fear. I will not comment further on the (mainly ecological) recent turns in social thought that motivate new transcendental dialectical critical realist notions in 3L.

Perhaps the key theoretical notions in the realm of 3L are those of internal relationality and holistic causality. An element A is internally related to B if B is a necessary condition for the existence of A, whether this relation is reciprocal, symmetrical or not. Internally related elements may be said to be 'intra-active'. Intra-action (including holistic causality) occurs among internally related elements in three basic modes: (1) existential constitution (which includes existential constitution by (a) totalities and (b) geo-historical rhythmics), in which one element is essential and intrinsic to another; (2) permeation, in which one element contains another; and (3) connection, in which one element is merely causally aefficacious on the other. In its simplest form, holistic causality may be said to operate when a complex coheres in such a way that (a) the totality, i.e. the form or structure of the combination, causally co-determines the elements; and (b) the form and structure of the elements causally co-determine each other, and so causally co-determine the whole. But this notion may be generalised to include heterocosmic causality; this is causality which includes reversed, amplified, magnetic, quantum and other holistic-like and reflexive processes and effects. This includes spread, split-and-combined, multiple and other differentiated and unevenly distributed causal relations and links, such as those which are involved in *karma* (which is intrinsically holistic and 'quantised').

Dialectical critical realism opposes dialectical universalisability and concrete universality to the abstract universalisability and universality (and objectivity) of analytical (or expressivist) thought. Dialectical and concrete universality and universalisability are consistent with, indeed imply, the concrete singularity of the individuals concerned. This necessitates, as I have shown in *DPF* (see 2.7), a four-term analysis of universalisability = singularity. I have already discussed the topic of constellationality in 1.2 above, in the context of the stratification of being. As for the key concept of identity, this must be understood in the context of entity relationism. This incorporates, essentially, an understanding of the formation of the nature of beings in the context of their geo-historical rhythmics and their internal relations with other beings with which they have holistic, including stratified (1M) and processual (2E)[50] or similar (for example, heterocosmic or otherwise reflexive) relations. Above all, we must avoid the mistake of thinking of the identity of a thing as being fixed. Things, especially human subjects, are involved in dialectical learning processes; they are essentially in development and in a process of becoming, albeit perhaps in the process of becoming what they already essentially are. Indeed, the orientation of the dialectic of shedding suggests that this process of becoming may well be in the direction of greater simplicity, of the freeing of the soul or self from heteronomous or extraneous determinations, from the hitherto intrinsic outside or the legacy of the presence of the past. But this process of liberation or autonomisation can only be thought in the context of a shedding situated by concepts such as entity relationism, processual formation, combined and uneven production, spread distribution, collective causality, event-as-a-totality,[51] and so on.

I have already argued that the antinomies of philosophy are to be explained by multiple alienations at all four planes and all dimensions or levels of social being, and ultimately in terms of alienation from Self, God, Totality, cosmos and so on. This alienation results in ontological insecurity or fear and manifests itself *inter alia* in ontological monovalence. I will be brief in this section because I will be considering the nature of the self *inter alia* in the context of the dialogue between Krishna and Arjuna on the Field of Kurukshetra, which grounds the resolution of the problem of agency – what is to be done? (or what am I to do?) – in a radical reconsideration of the nature of the self and prescribes dialectics of inaction and action to achieve the equanimity and poise necessary for dharmic or spontaneous right action. Second, I will be reconsidering it in detail in the narrative of this book in the context both of four-planar social being and of the dialectics of self-realisation or liberation, including the dialectics necessary for the emancipation of our capacities or powers for spontaneous right or dharmic action.

I need to say something more about the dialectics of desire and fear; and the contrast between love, that is, unconditional love, and fear. Love unites, heals and

50 It is important to stress that the 3L realm of totality incorporates the results of 1M and 2E; and, in the human world, also of 4D.

51 See p. 28 above.

expands; fear divides, wounds and contracts. Only unconditional love does so however unconditionally, without karmically binding the agent to the world in which his action occurs. Conditional love is fear-based. Desire and fear are both forms of and are driven by incompleteness, the alienation from self (and the autonomy or self-sufficiency it would provide), producing ontological insecurity and requiring completion by an object. Love is subject-referential; fear and desire are object-referential. It is the negative state that focuses *attention* that generates the desire or the fear so that whether the intentional state of awareness is the positive one of desire or the negative one of fear it is motivated by fear not unconditional love in both cases. (Conditional love is love motivated by fear, for example, of loss.) Fear and desire mutually imply each other and are real perspectival switches on each other. Thus fear is just desire to avoid the situation feared and desire is just fear of not possessing the object, situation etc. desired. So fear and desire mutually imply each other and both are grounded in ontological insecurity, i.e. alienation of self from Self. The focus of the attention on the negative state which motivates the desire or the fear results in the tendency for that negative state to be realised so that fear and/or desire are both tendentially self-undermining, tending to produce the state feared or reproduce the state of desire, the state in which the emotion is expressed. Of course if the desire happens to be realised or the feared situation avoided, this merely results in the generation of another desire or another situation to be afraid of. In this way the emotional pattern is repeated. At the same time, intention to realise the desire or to avoid the fear binds the agent karmically to the world so that the desire or fear persists as something that must be realised or faced in a future life. Desire, fear and conditional love and other negative or less than fully autonomous emotions – the only appropriate emotional response to life on earth is joy or unconditional love – generates the theorems of the mutual implication of fear and desire, and of the treble futility of desire, fear and other negative emotions. Thus they tend to be (1) self-undermining; (2) self-reproductive; and (3) clinging, that is, karmically binding the agent to their realisation or the realisation of that object on to which the attachment or aversion is now displaced. However, the dialectic of fear or desire, which is at best a dialectic of conditional (not unconditional) love, indexed to attachment, although immediately nugatory, does initiate its own sublation, namely in the dialectic of desire (or attachment) to freedom (without attachment) through the extension to it (but still via the inexorable logic of dialectical universalisability) I have rehearsed in section 2. Indeed, the chief mechanism of the karmic learning process is the dialectic of the desire for freedom which is a dialectic of self-realisation and ultimately of God-realisation, that is, a mechanism for a radically re-enchanted reality.

4 4D: Transformative praxis or creative work

The transition to 4D has been made from the conception of the self as stratified, rhythmically developing and concretely singularised/individuated; as elastic, expanding, shifting. It is imortant to note that it is not just the concept of the self, or even consciousness of the self, but the self itself that is expanding. This new concept of the self is grounded in the 2E dialectical critique of analytical reasoning incorporating a critique of the traditional, analytical subject–predicate form, which presupposes fixed entities abstracted from their (developing and structured) contexts; and it results in concepts of self-negation incorporating developmental, including specifically radical, negation. Selves have an intrinsic nature and from their intrinsic nature flows their *dharma*. Action in accordance with their *dharma* is spontaneous right action, least effort action (the sun does not try to shine, it just shines) and maximally coherent. Coming from the widest possible vantage point, from the level of the transcendent, it is maximally creative. Informed by that widest possible vantage point, it is also maximally compassionate. Thus it is selfless but Self-centred. It serves humanity and has maximum evolutionary potential both for the self and for others. This is the free liberated action of an individual or being as thus-formed, that is as formed (concretely singularised) the way it is; and it consists in action in accordance with its nature or real essence. So the resolution of the problem of agency is grounded in a radically tranformed conception of the self, of being and of identities. What I am to do depends upon my *dharma*, i.e. my intrinsic (concretely singularised) nature. This will be spontaneous right action. The question of agency therefore depends on resolution of the question of the self. Moreover, the *dharma* of a being is objective. This raises the possibility of an objective morality, though specific moral judgements will always have to be concretely singularised and sensitised on a two-way basis. For agents stand in differential relations to each other; and the best (or right) thing for A to say to B is not necessarily any more the right thing for C to say to B than is it generally right that A and B and C should all do the same thing in the same circumstances. Each person's *dharma* is unique.

I turn now briefly to the topic of dialectics of self-realisation. Dialectics of self-realisation can be divided into two kinds: dialectics of inaction and dialectics of action. The dialectics of inaction are four-fold: (1) the dialectic of ontological access or grace; (2) the dialectic of purification or shedding (that is the elimination of heteronomous and unnecessary orders of determination), this is the dialectic of letting go of excess baggage, *karma*, the presence of the past, habitual dispositional routines ingrained as impulsions or compulsions; (3) the dialectic of embodiment, this is infusion of the dialectic of access and the results of the dialectic of shedding (or clearing or releasing or letting go) so that it permeates all aspects of the totality of one's being; and (4) the dialectic of witnessing-in-activity.[52] These dialectics of inaction are all in the vertical, or self→Self direction of expansion.

The dialectics of action consist in (5) the dialectic of praxis and non-attachment of intentional, engaged but unattached, activity-in-the-world; and (6) the dialectic of desire for freedom. As already seen this dialectic has two movements, first to individual self-realisation and second to universal self-realisation (or God-realisation in one sense of that term). The first aspect of the second movement along the other or horizontal planes of the social cube and taken to its highest level results in 'God-consciousness', just as the dialectics of inaction lead to cosmic consciousness. The dialectic of desire for freedom, however, as we have seen, logically leads to the position that only a universalised state of non-attachment, that is, of intentional activity without attachment to results or consequences, a generalised state of desirelessness can lead to the satisfaction of all desires and an end to all suffering rooted in the alienation of men from their selves, each other and the cosmos as a whole (aspects of the God within and the God without). Only such a situation is indefinitely sustainable. This is the inexorable end, then, of the dialectic of desire for freedom, a dialectic which leads to freedom without desire or attachment, aversion or fear, insecurity or heteronomous orders of determination. The dialectic of the desire to freedom thus fuses with (7) the dialectic of love, solidarity and compassion (through collective and totalising agency). They may be resumed in (8) in a dialectic of philosophical recapitulation or self-consciousness. Implementing these dialectics of action and inaction involves dialectics of yoga and *yagya*, and of absolute and relative being; and inscribed within these are also dialectics of inner and outer fulfilment, and along the characteristic two orientations (vertical and horizontal of the social cube) dialectics, of the development of levels of transcendental, cosmic, God and unity consciousness. The move from individual to universal self-realisation may be seen first as a *project* as on the programme of the Bodhisattva or that of the dialectic of compassion encompassing all the stadia of four-planar social being, until it is seen under the aspect of absolute spirit in unity consciousness and thence on to the actualisation or realisation of the project of universal self-realisation in unity existence or God-realisation in one inflexion of that term. Then there is the dialectic of levels of realised being, first freedom from the creation of new *karma*; second freedom from the effects of past *karma*; through to identity, manifestation or realisation of one's own Godness.

When we turn to the social cube in four-planar social being we see that, in the light of the further transcendentalisation of dialectical critical realism, it must be generalised. So we have the notion of putatively multi-dimensional human being

52 This goes hand in hand with the dialectic of subjectual, objectual and relational consciousness.

physically embedded in four-planar social space. This is consistent with the possibility of levels of being and embodiment not currently normally available to human sense-experience but causally efficacious and real none the less. So we can imagine a concept or conceptualise an inner funnel channeling down on (d) in four planar social space.[53] This is the human funnel; and we can be alienated at (d) from consciousness of levels of embodiment other than the physical just as we may be alienated from our essential self. Similarly, we may be alienated or less than fully integrated at differential levels of our physical constitution (for example, in the alignment of the energy centres known as the *chakras*).[54] The emphasis on (d) that is the primacy of the autoplastic moment in the dialectical coincidence of autoplastic and aleoplastic moments in the dialectic of transform*ed* transformative praxis stems from the fact that all change begins with and consists in work *at* the self even if all change does not consist in work *on* the self. This is an important point, so I will repeat it: all change then consists in work at, though not necessarily in work on, the self. Furthermore for both reduced self-alienation and greater efficiency (or aefficacy) in work on objects of work, generally, one must work on the self, that is work *at* (d) *on* (d). So, leading on from this we have the theorem that all change or at least all radical change, that is all creative change, begins with self-change, that is with a prior (analytically and/or chronologically) transformation in one's transformative praxis. Moreover all change also in a certain sense consists in (or involves) self-expansion. Thus one changes society by first (and also) changing oneself. Towards the end of the book, I will make explicit the similarities between Marx's critique of political economy and a Vedantian critique of the myopic world of avidyaic dualism. The clue to the unity of the two lies in an understanding of the significance of co-existence of autonomous and heteronomous determinations, and a conception in which liberation is conceived as involving the disemergence of the latter kind. With such disemergence comes true autonomy or Self-determination, an autonomy screened, and drained in the illusory but (demi-)real world of appearance and everyday life.

I have already hinted in section 1.2 above that the development of realism essayed here makes possible a re-evaluation of the old dispute between idealism and materialism, in which it is shown that only TDCR (that is, a transcendental dialectical critical realism) can avoid a dualistic split between agency and agent, and, shortly following on from such a split, further splits within both the agent and the action themselves. All this allows a reassessment of the role of ideas and intentional states in personal and social geo-history. Capitalism at the moment is

53 *DPF* 2.9, p. 160 and *passim*.

54 Thus we will see in the book how energy may be blocked (in part) at one *chakra* or cease to flow into another. Fully autonomous, non-alienated human being is also fully integrated and fully embodied human being.

the dominant world order. It is however faced with two pressing contradictions. A rising organic composition of nature threatens to tear the world itself apart with ecological contradictions. But a rising organic composition of ideas, dependent ultimately upon a rising organic composition of the transcendent (that is, of creativity in human life), makes possible the idea of a new organisation of the social world in keeping with, and attuned to, universal self-realisation and harmony. For it is upon the creativity of labour power, that is the creativity of man, that capitalism ultimately depends; and if the argument of this book is correct, this depends at least in essence upon immersion or absorption in (or other aefficacious access to) the absolute or the transcendent. Those at peace with themselves will thus naturally tend to be most creative. And those at peace with themselves will be most naturally compassionate, i.e. peaceful towards others. They will also be the most coherent, i.e. evolutionary and totalising in their thought and in their practice. Inner peace may therefore be the key to outer peace and the salvation of the planet. In thinking therefore of a topic of the rise and fall of the West, it may be not so much a question of thinking of the overreaching of the Western economies and societies by geographically Eastern ones, as the infusion of world hegemonic Western and capitalist ways of thinking and being with ideas traditionally associated with the East. If I am right, however, in the narrative of this book, these ideas and ways of being are not the prerogative of the East. They are equally consonant with both the teaching of the Christ and the whole thrust of the radical egalitarian libertarian tradition that incorporates both Rousseau and Marx. A new synthesis is what is required; and it is this new synthesis which this book attempts to initiate. Such a synthesis will see a partial rapprochment of the best insights of the New Age and the New Left movements, but such insights will be set in a context of a global philosophy which resonates with themes traceable back to the dawn of the great world civilisations (and perhaps even beyond).

II

ODYSSEY OF A SOUL

1

TO THE PROMISED LAND

Life One: Crossing the Red Sea with Moses – the Teacher

(1) A dreamy (and somewhat wild – a wildness which will explode into anger in L7) child, in tune with nature spirits and angels, somewhat alone (= all one), crosses the Red Sea, at the age of seven, with his father and mother and siblings (of whom he is very close to a tomboy sister (Ma)[1]). So dreamy is he in fact that he needs to be constantly grounded and regrounded by his kindly and understanding father (Fg).

(2) He learns his father's trade as a potter, but his father, Moses and others quickly see his spiritual potential, and in particular that his vocation is to be an enlightened and enlightening spiritual teacher. He successfully negotiates and passes all twelve initiations. He becomes very strong physically and mentally, perfectly balanced with a deep mind and a great, warm open heart. His third eye is open and he is inspired by (visions of) angels and the visitations of enlightened masters and other holy beings. He is guided terrestrially (on the physical plane) by a wizened old man (M), a close colleague of Moses who becomes his spiritual teacher at the age of twelve and who supervises his various initiations at the ages of twelve, nineteen and so on. He is utterly devoted to this teacher, and (as predicted) he will eventually succeed him.

(3) At the age of twelve, a significant incident occurs. He drops a precious earthenware water jug and it fragments into twelve pieces. This *water* jug is a symbol both of purity (water) and of the age of Aquarius (the water pourer) into which we are now entering (the moment of repurification or of shedding (heteronomous determinations). It also symbolises that the soul will have to meet with and encounter impurity (and repurify) in order to realise its mission. Water

1 This is a character and a motif which will recur. It signifies an ideal disinterested totality in comparison with the more difficult relations between (1) husband and wife or more generally lovers and (2) parents and children – more generally teachers.

is also a symbol of the angelic essence covering (like a *veil*) God. The twelve pieces can signify the twelve initiations, twelve tribes of Israel, twelve signs of the zodiac, twelve disciples or whatever (including 'the twelve steps to heaven' discussed in section 1.4 of Part I).[2] He is utterly crestfallen and has to be consoled by his father, who points out to him the transience of all things (save spirit or God); that is, all things terrestrial. This is the first definition of the distinction between the *absolute* (characterised by permanence, unchange and not subject to the law of *karma*, cause and effect) and the *relative* (characterised by transience, repetition, dependent origination and combined co-production and governed by quantum natural law, characterised by overlapping and uneven succession in time and spread distributions in space) and of the perils of an *attachment*, the ultimate cause of all suffering.[3] The significance of the jug, bowl or vessel is that it is the *hole* (absence, emptiness, cavity, space) that makes it such, and keeps it *whole*. Without it, there is no whole. And if you break it, you lose both hole and whole. This is the first lesson in the (normatively) positive/negative *duality of absence* and of the complementarity of 2E, the realm of absence and negativity and 3L, the realm of totality and holism. And the story related in this book is really one about *alienation* and its overcoming or transcendence, ultimately only in (universal) self-transcendence (enlightenment) or universal Self-realisation in 'unity existence'. For the driving impulse of the dialectic described in the book is to produce for *everyone* now a *total* philosophy for the *whole* of their (i.e. everyone's) being; and it is this drive or inspiration which animated L1 and animates the present writer now. There is completion (wholeness) at the beginning and at the end of the story.[4]

Later in his life, in a significant reprise of this event, he in turn will have to console his favourite and eldest son, the apple of his eye, when, at a similar age, he in turn drops a valuable pot (is it one of his father's creations or the chalice

2 If the story is considered to begin in Chapter 2 with the encounter between L14 and L2, it can also signify the twelve lives between them (including L1, considered as a flashback from L2 in Palestine).

3 It is *maya*, the veil of illusion, that produces spiritual myopia (as in Plato's allegory of the cave (or our relatively (necessary) use of sun (soul) shades; and the sun as symbolic of alethic truth in so many, including Zoroastrian and Essene, cultures), to mistake the ephemeral for the alethic, transitory attachments for permanent peace.

4 The topic of alienation also relates to the so-called 'Jewish question', the esoteric significance of the fragmented pot or jug: a split between the chosen people and the rest of mankind, leading to fragmentation, diaspora, persecution, holocaust and war(s) (including world war). More generally, instead of the split between two kinds of soul – (α), those subject to God's grace, and (β), those not so subject to God's grace – we can affirm the essential *unity* of mankind and universality of enlightenment given by the universal ingredient categorial structure of man as God. For its part the resolution of the related aporia of free will and determinism (and the rejection of the idea of pre-determinism) is given by recognition of (1) the reality of free will and (2) the realisation that, as *thus-formed*, we are most free when we act in accordance with our intrinsic nature or concretely singularised *dharma*.

representing the holy grail, that M, his teacher, has given him?), scattering it likewise into twelve fragments. (And neither is this the only time that this motif will recur in this book.) This is the wheel of life (the potter's wheel, and the circle of the book), and shows the transitoriness of relative being, the falsity (nullity, myopia) of attachment to material things (including symbols) and the essential unity of life (including its essential constitution by absence, the space between, the *gap* as container and the absenting necessary for the creation (and continued being) of any conceivable coherent presence).

(4) I have already mentioned his spiritual teacher (M), the wizened old man to whom he is utterly devoted. This man tells him that he will eventually succeed him. The old man teaches, as he will in his turn teach, in small groups of three or four, the esoteric teachings of the perennial wisdom. In these circles reincarnation and *karma* are taken for granted.[5]

M gives him a *chalice* as a *symbol* of his coming, eventual, enlightenment at the age of thirty-three/four. (Thus the holy grail as symbol of enlightenment, eternal life or freedom, i.e. autonomy or self-determination.) Is this the chalice that his firstborn breaks? A symbol of the fall consequent upon engagement in the things of the world (on the physical plane), on the path of the householder, rather than the recluse, the path of action rather than that of inaction (renunciation) involving as it does (or at the very least, seems to do) so intrinsically sexuality, money, boundaries, property (possessions), having and losing (rather than just being), and all manner of attachments and aversions, cravings and suffering. The path is indeed perfectly spiritual in L1, to be recaptured in L15 in and with the cup of superabundance from superconsciousness (the holy grail or enlightenment, eternal life or freedom). He repairs the chalice; thus-formed and trans-formed.[6]

M also gives him (L1) a *staff* which the old man materialises (or appears to materialise) out of thin air, as a proleptic symbol of the coming journeys West to East (in L2, L5 and L6, also L15) and East to West (L7–(and especially L11)–L15). (This staff will also become in a sense a pen; and in L5 it symbolises the cross. In L3 it appears as a rod and in L7 as a sword.)

At any rate, L1 becomes a spiritual teacher at the age of twenty-six. But then, when he is in his mid-thirties, his own teacher, the old man M, dies. He is distraught, inconsolable, despite everything his father (and others, including especially

5 Some of them believe they initially came from India. See the splits and syntheses thematised in L11 and L15.

6 In the chalice he burns incense. It is rediscovered in Alexandria in L2; he will fill it with water and place in it a rose, to give to his love in L2. It is the reflection of this rose in water that L9 sees as he dies (see the cover of the book), and the dancing rose in L12 that symbolises enlightenment. (L14 loses his love in America and wishes her ashes to be scattered with roses in the Atlantic, thus purging the memory of Atlantis in L3.)

his sister) can say to and do for him. One morning he climbs up into the mountains, where his teacher lived in a cave. (Why a cave? Why do holy men live in caves?[7]) His teacher suddenly appeared (materialised) in front of him – did his teacher rephysicalise (resurrect) himself or was L1 just able to see and communicate with him astrally? – and talks to him for a good hour. The astral world, he tells him, contains everything that the physical world does but much else besides; and reality itself is far greater than even the astral world, so that we have the situation: the domain of the real contains but is not exhausted by the domain of the astral, which in turn contains but is not exhausted by the domain of the physical, which can be represented by the formula $d_r \geq d_a \geq d_p$.[8] Consciousness, and being generally, is a continuum and we normally experience only its most gross or elementary aspects. In our first, most essential reality we are immortal and at one with God.

When his teacher leaves him, elated and re-empowered,[9] he rushes down the mountain, crying gleefully 'He lives! He lives!' This commences the driving impulse of the book – love for, and desire to be one with, the divine – the desire besides and by which all other desires and ultimately itself (for when it is achieved, it is no longer desire but reality) fade or pale into insignificance. Union with the beloved! the cosmic beloved, the Lord.

(5) Meanwhile at the age of twenty-two/three he has married (MgE). In a colourful ceremony pink and white flowers are scattered like (what they are in effect) confetti. He is happily married and he and his wife have three children: his eldest son, who follows him as both a potter and a teacher – in his case, of the unconverted (something that our soul does not begin to do until L5[10]) – a daughter whom he adores and a younger son of a somewhat rebellious and sullen nature to whom he finds it difficult to relate.

(6) Meanwhile his psychic powers and intellectual and intuitive gifts are developing apace; he teachers the esoteric wisdom and occult sciences and arcane arts, including especially numerology and astrology. And, possessing a way with words, as his elders quickly realised, he is sent, under cover of being a trading potter, as an envoy to the neighbouring territories to meet other leaders and liaise with other Israelite tribes and communities. By his mid-forties, already a voracious reader of books, he is starting to write his own compendium of spiritual philosophy. Finally in his mid-fifties he succeeds to his spiritual teacher's position

7 But not only holy men. See Plato's allegory already referred to in footnote 3, above.

8 See $d_r \geq d_a \geq d_e$ discussed in section 1.2 of Part I.

9 Something like this will occur in L5 with Jesus and in L2 with Buddha, the vision of Krishna and the dream of Laozi.

10 But we should note here that this is also partially an effect of a structural feature; namely that Christianity is the first main proselytising, actively universalising religion or world view.

and comes to live in that holy cavernous mountain habitat in which his mentor dwelt, descending from it from time to time to teach, or for discussions or meetings and celebrations (festivals, concerts and the like). Close to God and integrated his life is full of joy, the only appropriate emotional response to life on earth. Full of happiness and laughter, he appears with twinkling eyes always laughing, joking, even a bit of a prankster. At one with his community (although his community is at odds with others) he joins with his tomboy sister, long since happily married herself, to organise concerts with music, singing and dancing, including belly dancing of a primitive form brought over from Egypt. However there is also something wild, elemental and Dionysian about his love for God, his people and the elements of nature. The totality here is almost too undifferentiated, too primitive, not yet informed by the experiences, trials and tribulations of L2–L14.

He partly recounts and partly fabricates stories – of Egypt, the crossing, far off parts – for his children and grandchildren (and their friends). He invents vivid fairy stories, and adventure stories too. He is a born storyteller, still dwelling in part in the reverie, world of dreams of his youth. Indeed, he becomes a bit of a 'tribal' storyteller or myth maker, conceiving myth as merely an allegorical form of truth or rather, in describing the possible (and perhaps on some other higher plane in some manner or mode occurent), as higher in truth-value (or, we could say, truth-potential) than the actual narrative of geo-history. (This, then, is the thesis of the primacy or prior truth of myth or legend over actualised history to which all societies in their actual cosmogenies tend to subscribe.) We see him with his daughter (B) sending her to sleep with his stories, nestling her in his arms, while she holds on to her toys, a little painted wooden camel doll and a potter's artefact, a spinning top.

Finally after fifteen years as successor to his spiritual teacher M in his position, he dies peacefully in his sleep.

(7) *Conversations with God* (by Neale Donald Walsch) argues that instead of the 'ten commandments', God is best seen as commending to Moses and his (the chosen) people 'ten commitments'. At play here is the dialectic between an external and an internal law, the God within and the God without, and a tension between a religion of observation of rituals and rites and externally imposed injunctions and a religion of a loving heart. But if God is the ultimate categorial structure of the world, then the God within is at one with the God without and any inner conflict, any absence of full installation of the inner God (the God within), will result in alienation, including lack of (internal) integration (e.g. of the *chakras*) and external fulfilment (including external flourishing). This secret doctrine of the constellational unity of the inner and the outer (with the outer as constellationally englobing the inner) was well known to the initiates who taught our soul. So the dilemma of Judaism is resolved. The God without is to be

(already is constellationally included in) the God within; and this God within is within *all*, actually (though occludedly, and overlain by extraneous, heteronomous determinations), grounding the essential and potential unity of mankind. The role of practice/discipline is to replace fear and rote by love and spontaneity, external obedience by inner obedience and thence by intuition and spontaneous right action. Dedication to God's law (word, message or representative(s)) gives way to love of God, which in turn gives way to unity with God, at which point the God within is (or has already been) realised by shedding the veils which obscure and dislocate it.

In sum, then, L1 resolves the dilemmas of Judaism. The God without is to constellationally include the God within. All souls are concretely singularised and all communities are particularised. But this is underscored by the essential Godlike unity of man. The role of practice is to prepare the ground for an ethic of unconditional and spontaneous love. But L1 is in a sense too undifferentiated (unmediated) and too particularistic (under-universalised); also in a sense too wild, too dreamy, too 'astral', too ethereal or mythic, too committed to the primacy of the imaged (whether real or imaginary) over the actual and insufficiently concrete.[11] It will have to be followed by a much more physical, more variegated but universalising life. So the action moves on a millennium or so to Ancient Greece at the time of Pythagoras, a contemporary of Buddha among others.

11 Thus: is the crossing real or metaphorical or both? Is M himself an 'aspect' of Moses or merely a colleague, disciple (pupil) or follower of Moses or (again) both?

2

PART A
UNDER THE STARS: RE-ENCHANTING REALITY

Life Two: In Ancient Greece I – the Philosopher – from Pythagoras to Laozi

A French philosopher and university professor, mystic and doctor peers into the night sky with his telescope seeking out stars light years away. It is the mid-1930s (CE). Like Kant, he is awed by the starry heavens above (and though not perhaps so much by the moral law as the mighty oceanic depths within). In particular, as an avid reader of H.G. Wells, he is fascinated by time travel. On the stars he is looking at now he can see (or could see if his telescope were powerful enough) events which on those stars took place hundreds of thousands of years ago (the time it takes the light – which moves with a finite velocity – to travel back to earth). If only we could get sufficiently far from where we are now (or travel sufficiently quickly, faster than the speed of light[1]) then perhaps we could now see the Ancient Greek world as it was then.

What was it like, for instance, in Pythagoras' time? Is Pythagoras still writing, teaching and contemplating even now? Or can we perhaps see him as such, now, even though it no longer is, but was actually then? He leaves his balcony, spinning with these thoughts, draws his shutters and begins to chant the sound of God, intoning the mantra 'Om' (or alternating it with the sequence 'om, ah, hum') in the way his meditation teacher and guru, Paramahansa Yogananda, has taught him. A feeling of peace – of restful alertness – descends upon him, pervading his being. Often in this state he can see angels in the clouds, fairies in the fields (which he has tried not very successfully to photograph, the camera not being, so to speak, in that state), sprites dancing in the flames of fire, holy beings such as Buddhas besporting themselves and scenes (like the Last Supper) portrayed vividly

1 If perhaps the speed of thought were infinite, instantaneous. See Empedocles's vision of a 'holy mind, darting through the whole cosmos with rapid thoughts'.

in the water, faces and figures, some primordial, some pretty, laced in granite in rocks. Consciousness, life and the hand of God seem to be present everywhere, in the naturalistic and surrealistic paintings of friends, in the furniture, just everywhere. Oh, to have a time machine. Suddenly he is aware of an expansion of sensation in his brow. Suddenly he finds himself hurtling through time into the past: his third eye is his (space–)time machine.

He (L14 of the present book) is back in the Ancient Greek world in the days of Pythagoras in the sixth century BCE. He homes in on a young man (L2 in the present book, a millennium after L1 during which a dozen lives which need not detain us now have occurred). The young man he is witnessing is strangely similar yet utterly different, destined to become like him a philosopher, teacher and explorer, but two and a half millennia ago. Intrigued by what he sees of his life, he eventually begins to talk to him, to question him, inviting him into his study, where the whole vast panorama (and in a certain sense the rest of the book) unfolds.[2]

(1) Who is this philosopher? Like L14, but under the influence of Orpheus and Pythagoras rather than Hegel and Marx, a richly endowed, expansive mind roams the skies at night and ponders their meaning by day. Like L14, he is always on the move. Thus he travels west to Italy to be with Pythagoras (who has migrated there from Samos); south to Egypt, where he is fascinated by the ancient civilisations and comes across remnants of buried Atlantis; north to the various Greek settlements and colonies; and most momentously, east to Babylon, Persia and India (where he learns of Krishna, Buddha – and Laozi). Languages come to him easily. He teaches dialectic, ontology and phronesis, and he investigates all the mysteries known to man of being. He predicts eclipses and earthquakes, he argues and heals, uses symbols and signs and he is never still: a bumble bee. He sees himself as completing (or at least building on) the work of Pythagoras by bringing the wisdom of the East back to the West. (This is the first journey from East to West in the book.)

(2) Born in mainland Greece, in a settlement close to Athens to an aristocratic family, he finds himself restricted by his family and immediate circle. Going to school in Athens, where he falls under the spell of a Socratic figure to whom he is deeply attached, frees him up a bit. But he does not see eye to eye with his father, who has in mind a military life for him (anathema to the young philosopher) and has lined up an arranged marriage for him to consolidate an intra-aristocratic alliance. This he resists, with some backing from his mother (from whom when young he constantly seeks protection and favour, but from whom only a measure is forthcoming; in fact, the only member of his immediate

2 Was L1 then just a mythopoetic dream?

family he gets on with is his sister, who shares his love of music and to whom he will be close throughout most of his long life). Thus much to the annoyance and chagrin of his father, who regards him as effeminate and unmanly, not so much on account of his friendship with older men but because of the type (spiritual, musical) he consorts with. Still – the only saving grace – his son does excel in sports, competing regularly in Olympiad-type games.

(3) Contrary to his father's wishes, he leaves the mainland not for a military career but for Croton in southern Italy, where he joins Pythagoras' community. He is ecstatic. For the first time there he feels truly at home. The nights and days, the discussions and celebrations have a magical quality about them. He quickly excels himself in philosophy; and he takes naturally to all the practices and customs of Pythagorean communal life, to vegetarianism and so on. He absorbs himself in philosophy and the occult mysteries, in which he quickly establishes himself as an apprentice master. He enjoys music and dancing (inviting his sister to the community for a spell). 'Bliss it was in that dawn to be alive.' He becomes very fond of many of his teachers, and to Pythagoras himself he is completely devoted. After a year or two, Pythagoras summons him to his room and tells him that one day he will become a great teacher in his own right, but first he needs to travel – particularly east to India, where he will bring back the teachings of great beings (Krishna and Buddha, especially). He will bring back an ethic of engaged unattached activity in the world, that is, an ethic of neither attachment (the fallacy of the path of action) nor that of disengagement (the fallacy of the path of renunciation). But first he must return to Greece to bid farewell to his parents. Though sad to leave his teachers, he has the urge to travel in his bones and he readily acquiesces to his master's plans.

(4) Returning to his family home to bid farewell to his parents, he finds his father still only partially reconciled to his *philosophia* – love of wisdom – and he rejects the elaborate escorting caravan of retainers, animals and foodstuffs that his mother has prepared for him and sets out on his journey with minimum attendance. He heads first for Alexandria, which is already a bustling cosmopolitan city and already has a great library. Here he is befriended by a trader (who subsequently takes advantage of him) who says he will arrange his eastbound trip. It is here that he finds the chalice; or is it a magic lantern? He falls passionately in love with the trader's daughter (T), and for six–eight months they are inseparable. She is the true love of his life; but they realise they cannot marry. Her father has other plans for her. So L2, after travelling extensively further south up the Nile valley, being particularly impressed by the sacred sites of Phebes (and the memories they seem to afford of distant pasts) and exploring varied texts there and back in Alexandria (and from them and in subsequent discussions learning the terrible fate of Atlantis, with its sombre warning as we stand on the precipice of the third millennium of the common era), must continue his eastward mission. So

he travels on through Babylon, with a detour to Palestine, which evokes happy memories of L1, and into Persia, where he encounters Zoroastrianism and precursors of Manichaeism. Throughout his trip he is keeping a meticulous and engrossing diary. One Persian incident, where he again falls in love (the love to cure his heartache), is significant. Once more he breaks an earthenware jug, while absent-mindedly washing himself in the morning, smashing it into twelve fragments. *Déjà vu*.

(5) Continuing his journey, he moves on through the Khyber Pass on to the plains of Punjab and across to, in and around north India. The Aryan Brahmin civilisation – with its infrastructure of rites and rituals (*yagya*) – is flourishing. He becomes familiar with the Upanishads and the six main schools of Indian philosophy: Nyaya (logic), Vaisesika, Sankhya, Yoga, Mimamsa and Vedanta (in which he is engrossed). He comes across an early version of the *Gita* and becomes enchanted with it. He sees a magical performance of the *Mahabharata* and becomes captivated by Krishna's dialogue with Arjuna. He has painstakingly taught himself Sanskrit (and Pali) and the other Indian tongues he needs to get by. And then he comes across the great ferment created by the Buddha's recent teachings. He seeks out and finds the Buddha. He listens to him preach a doctrine of phronesis. As he listens he feels (not for the last time) the Buddha's heartbeat pulsating in his own heart. He also investigates Jainism. Then, carrying voluminous notes (of Buddha's oral teachings and everything he has learnt and experienced on his trip), some Upanishads and a treasured *Gita*, he begins his return journey. He falls ill, stays in the foothills of the Himalayas, falls in love with the daughter (Md) of the Kshatriya family who tend him and (this time) gets married. Soon after this he has a vision of Krishna, who tells him his *dharma* is to bring together, unite, synthesise East and West. Krishna dances away in the night air. He recovers completely and prepares again to leave for home.

The French philosopher is now in ardent dialogue with the Greek philosopher. They discuss Greek, Indian and modern European philosophy. (In which world is the discourse taking place? It doesn't matter? Is the rest of the book taking place in his study? Is the reader in his study now, or is he in the reader's? Again, it doesn't matter. Not in the sense that there is no fact of the matter, but in the sense that the reader may take it either (or any) way.)

The French philosopher is seeing the manifestation of consciousness, especially faces, everywhere, in space, in clouds, carpets, cups of coffee. He is finding it ever easier to travel back and forth (at least up to the present) in time.

So L2 begins his journey home with his wife, who soon gives birth to a young child, having been summoned to attend the festivities surrounding his sister's daughter's marriage the following year. Before he can leave India, however, he has another amazing experience. Laozi appears to him in a dream and explains to him the principles of Taoist philosophy and the differences between his philosophy and that of Confucius. This fascinates the Greek philosopher, and he decides to prolong his stay in India to come to a more complete understanding of the main principles of oriental philosophies as they have come to him now. In the meantime his first-born child dies, and he becomes supremely aware of the fact of finitude, the finitude of earthly being. Pressed with requests to go home and eager to prolong his studies, he is now becoming fascinated with Mimamsa, in which ultimately everything of substance or value is seen as in heterocosmic affinity with the Vedas. At the same time he knows his real goal is enlightenment, that poise and equanimity of mind that belongs to the great ones he has encountered in his life: Pythagoras, Buddha, Krishna and perhaps Laozi. How can everything be achieved in such a small compass of time? He sets out once more for the Himalayas, this time in search of the renowned herbal drug *soma* (which is coincidentally the Greek for body), which is reputed to give immortal life. He finds it without too much difficulty and takes some back with him on his return trip to Greece. He returns home as rapidly as he can, and thence goes back to Croton, where he presents the old Pythagoras with his huge manuscripts. Besides philosophy, he has also taken back much medical knowledge, Indian epistemology and logic, linguistics, numerology, astrology and astronomy.

At this pivotal juncture, L14 sees two versions – in parallel, as on a split screen, of the rest of L2's life (equally confirmed by (and for that matter denied by the other) L2). On the first, his life is prolonged by the consumption of *soma*; so that we see him presenting a new edition of his manuscripts to Anaxagoras (who saw mind or *nous*, for the Vedics an effect or manifestation rather than the cause or source of consciousness, everywhere) and later still yet another edition to Socrates (with the young Plato in attendance, who is much impressed by the idea of the actuality of pre-enlightenment in the formulation of his subsequent doctrine of knowledge as amnesis or recollection). Eventually, however, the entropy of relative being outweighs the effects of the *soma* and he ages so much that, in a Chinese Taoist explosive–implosive transformation of a thing into its opposite, his death as an old man becomes his (re)birth as a young woman (see L3) – with what effects – in effect he has moved from the illusions of *soma* to the perils of attachment – and *karma* we shall see anon. On the second version of the rest of L2's life, he merely wearily continues his travels, both intellectual and physical.

(6) Thus he now goes about intellectually synthesising all these materials in a part Orphic–Pythagorean/part Indian way. He does this while travelling through the various Greek settlements dotted in and around the Mediterranean (after an initial period in south Italy as Pythagoras' *de facto* successor). He first establishes his own school in Athens, but it is too systematic and radical for the sophistic climate of the times. He then moves south with his Indian wife (Md) to establish a Pythagorean community near Polis in what is now Cyprus. Here a vain Greek princess (B) has come to the legendary reputed birthplace and home of

Aphrodite, Greek goddess of beauty. She is seeking, in a way like him, the secret of eternal youth or beauty, to match his search for eternal life (whether as absolute wisdom or through the infinite prolongation of physical life with *soma*). She visits him and has a brief affair with him. With her husband deceased in combat, she is in the habit of travelling with her tame leopards. One day while L2 is sleeping they gaily romp on his bed, causing considerable pain to his testicles. However later the same day he receives some oral concilation for this from the princess's daughter, who is to marry into the Alexandrian tradesman's family. Finally he moves up the Turkish coast with his wife to Ionia, where he seeks to establish an even purer community near Miletus, where he dies (here he hears stories that Thales had an Indian father and that Heraclitus too had travelled to India before him). Here he has chosen the path of renunciation; this will be lived out in even purer form in L3. But his whole message is that of the *Gita* and that of Buddha; of the fundamental identity of the two paths, of the *dharma*, imposed by one's *karma*. A Greek yogi, he will make the trips east again in L5 and L6, before in L7, and self-consciously in L11, commencing the reverse journey from east to west (a journey, both limbs of which will be undertaken in L15). Throughout L2 (mirroring in a sense the book itself) there is a dialectic of travel and rest, change and changelessness, the relative and the absolute. The only resolution of this dialectic is to become one with the absolute and at the same time ground the absolute (in thought, word and deed) in the flux of the here-and-now of the field of relativity. L2's search for a community, also to be frustrated in L3, and his desire for the transcendence of alienation at the various dimensions of the 'social cube' in 'four-planar social being', will eventually be gratified in L4.

Let me just at this juncture resume some of the main themes of the life of this Pythagorean philosopher:

1 Ontological realism (*inter alia* about God) combined with epistemological–experiential relativism, pluralism (tolerance, fallibilism and so on) encompassing the project of a synthesis of East and West and the idea (if not always its practice of) love and unity with the divine wherever it is found – whether, for instance, in India or in Greece.
2 The role of absence, the emptiness and the void (Laozi, and to an extent Buddha, versus Parmenides).
3 Dialectic, 2E, including reincarnation and *karma*.
4 The dialectic of self-realisation from empirical ego to transcendental Self and the requisite techniques of self-realisation.
5 An understanding of the goal of life as being to overcome split, alienation (ontological insecurity–fear–attachment and so on) and of techniques of self-realisation from dialectics of inaction including meditation etc. to dialectics of action, that is the yoga of action, practical skill in action, phronesis, including

the identity of spontaneous right, least effort and maximally coherent action, with the emphasis on the way of living as being effortlessly engaged, but unattached activity-in-the-world.

6 Non-violence (*ahimsa*, including vegetarianism).

7 A conception of laws as ordinarily understood, such as gravity, astrological tendency and so on, as transcendable by access to higher states of being; and of laws as stratified and transfactual in accordance with the stratification of being, in which the abolition of heteronomous orders of determination (themselves stratified) removes progressively inhibiting forms of constraint.

APPENDIX TO CHAPTER 2: PART A (L2)

Summary of and reflections on L2

The basic demarche of L2 is that he does not see knowledge as a practical affair; so he knows $_t$ but does not know $_p$ techniques of self-realisation, and consequently fails to embed the absolute in the relative.[1] Hence his incessant travel (failure to resolve the dialectic of activity and rest), in search of an unhypothetical, ideal, starting point and his refuge in *soma* as either (α) an extension to knowledge and/or (β) an extension to time.[2]

Second, L2 fails to achieve a harmonious social existence and travels from community to community, eventually setting up first one and then another of his own. At the root of this is the failure to let go, or even to appreciate – let alone clear – issues to do with sexuality, power, wealth and so on, which will come to the fore in L3. Behind the failure to let go (in L3 as in L2) is fear (overcome in L5, prepared by practice and loving service in L4).

Some important features of the philosophy L2 was to develop include:

1 Stratified monism; the reality of change and difference, space and time (including ontological realism and epistemological relativism) leading to the notion (in effect) of a concrete universal.
2 The emergent, though subordinate, reality of evil; and evil as dependent upon *avidya*; but *avidya* – both real, emergent and dependent upon incompleteness, alienation or lack – must be itself seen as a practical affair. Thus from (1) and (2) we have the view of the universe as a fundamentally harmonious whole leading to a stratified monism and with the harmoniousness of the whole qualified by the acceptance of the reality of evil.
3 The resolution of Parmenides' trilemma; but emptiness is everywhere or anywhere.

1 I will elaborate further on this in the interlude following Part B of Chapter 2.

2 See the significance of the Greek princess's search for eternal youth following Aphrodite's footsteps and their brief apocryphal encounter.

4 The ethic of engaged unattached activity; but he does not successfully engage it: he remains either attached or when unattached unengaged.
5 Dialectic and negativity (including the themes of reincarnation and *karma*) clearly related to Buddhist and Vedic teaching.
6 More specifically, his reception of Laozi's critique of Confucius and his own critical engagement with Sophists – in relation to performance and rhetorical success – and his hypothetical (or possible) influence on the young Plato.

The two ancient Greek philosophers who most influenced the young L2 were Pythagoras and Heraclitus. However, his ontology was neither as rarefied nor as bland as that of Pythagoras, nor was his monism as apparently materialistic as that of Heraclitus. Pythagoras had a view of the universe as an essentially harmonious whole, whereas Heraclitus' account, like that of Empedocles, stressed the reality of principles such as evil, strife, hatred, warfare as almost co-equal complements to good, right or love. What both Pythagoras' and Heraclitus' ontology had in common was however the idea of stratification. In Pythagoras' case, the stratification was of mathematical and musical scales, which for the young L2 through the repeated reapplication of the stratification of Pythagorian and more generally heterocosmic dyads (such as between the limited and limitless[3]) encouraged a view of reality itself as stratified in a multi-tiered way. If this was taken in combination with Heraclitus' principle that one should seek to explain surface change in terms of (relatively) unchanging underlying structure, it readily generated an immanent stratified ontology, similar to the one developed in section 1.2 of Part I. The stratification of immanent being in turn lent itself readily susceptible to the formulation of a doctrine of degrees of reality. But perhaps the most important consequence of the idea of the immanent stratification of being (in contradistinction to what I have called the Platonic/Aristotelian (transcendent/immanent) faultline) is to establish (a) the immanence, ingredience of God, including its grounding of the essential unity of man; and (b) the unity of what I have called the God within and the God without (that is the continuity of the cosmos, hence monism). If categorial realism establishes the ingredience of God; dispositional realism establishes the reality of the soul, and from (b) we already have its unity with God.

L2's attitude in respect of Parmenides' three ways – (a) being, (b) non-being and (c) seeming – was to accept the propriety of all three. Non-being was certainly necessary for any change, or difference, and hence for the establishment

3 As in Chinese *yin* and *yang*, Platonic forms and flux (or Aristotle's form and matter), Vedic bounded and unbounded and Buddhist void and phenomena. Heterocosmically related couples include part–whole, above–below, inner-outer, one-many and so on.

of any knowledge of being at all. On pain of sacrificing monism it therefore had to be included within ontology. Non-being in turn was not the same as semblance or illusion; and within the realm of semblance or illusion or what the Vedic tradition was to call *avidya* one had to distinguish objective from subjective semblance. Semblance moreover was part of reality itself, again on pain of sacrificing monism.

Maya, evil and so on (dependent upon, though not the same as, absence) are emergent, though subordinate, moments of stratified reality. So we have the idea of the reality of change and difference (including epistemic relativism) and error and evil as part of the relative world; and connectedly, the idea of the continuity of the absolute and the relative, including the demi-real, as all alike real; and hence the reality of both divine and earthly things, which indeed coincide in the categorial essence of man. It follows quickly from this that it is not contamination with the world as such, that is engagement in it, but attachment to or aversion from it, which is responsible for suffering and the round of reincarnation; so we have an ethic of engaged intentional but unattached activity in the world, where intentionality and attachment are seen as differentiated levels of emergence. So in opposition to Parmenides' three ways of being, non-being and seeming we have immanent being, stratified, mediated, relativised, concretised (concretely singularised) and the multi-tiered stratification of being punctuated with emptiness and absence (that is, with various degrees and kinds of void).

The crucial distinction here is between relative being and demi-reality, that is, the realm of *avidya*, *maya* or spiritual myopia within which correct judgements, perceptions and so on can be made or had. The aim of L2 is, via the dialectic of absolute and relative, to seek the permanent in change: to find a point of stability (which will also be a point of liberation or enlightenment) and a secure foundation for all sorts of error-free praxis or engagement in the world. The monist character of this construction comes out very clearly when we ask what are the relations between demi- and non-demi (either absolute or relative)-reality. *Avidya* depends upon truth, categorically presupposing it, while occluding, distorting or dislocating it, just as the totality of master–slave relationships depends on the creativity of slaves. Ignorance has as its tacit presupposition enlightenment and is powerless without it, that which it occludes.

In relation to the problem of good and evil, L2 seeks to find a *via media* between the blandness of Pythagoras and the Manicheanism (which had begun to flourish about that time further east) to which Heraclitus in his principles of love and strife and Empedocles in his principles of love and hate sailed very close. Evil was a real emergent dislocation of good, a warp, dependent upon our ignorance of it. Like most Greeks and like Buddha, virtue was seen as essentially a matter of the middle path between two extremes or vices. Basically, to act rightly was to act in accordance with one's *dharma* as 'thus-formed' (which will be acting in accordance with quantum natural law). But there are degrees of rightness of actions, and spontaneous right action or optimum action is only the limit in which we are completely at one with our *dharma* or our essential concretely singularised Godlike nature. Free will is real: we are free to act contrary to our nature and contrary to quantum natural law; and we do so act if we are informed by the myopia stemming from *avidya* or ignorance. One can act (do or say) anything one wants, but one cannot choose the consequences of one's actions, which are governed by natural law. What our L2 stresses against Pythagoras is the reality of evil as not just lack or privation or absence (though it depends upon these) but as an emergent power in its own right – though subordinate to good, right, Godliness – precisely as distortions, dislocations or deviations from it. In sum L2 sees the universe (1) as a harmonious whole or totality, but as (2) multi-tiered, stratified, immanent, characterised by degrees of relative endurance, difference, mediation and so on, and (3) as warped (containing falsity, ignorance, error, evil, vice) as emergent powers or rather products[4] of its stratified levels. The universe then is a harmonious whole or totality, but it is (a) stratified (the immanent stratification of being grounds the ingredience of God and the reality of the relative); (b) differentiated (thus the essential unity of man is subject to endless variety; see the concrete universal = concrete singular), and (c) warped (characterised by ills, evils and so on as subordinate distortions or dislocations of goods, truths and so on). Moreover, ontological realism *inter alia* about God is combined with (what L2 learns from his travels even if he was not already disposed to accept the thesis before) epistemological–experiential relativism, pluralism, fallibilism and so on. This implies *inter alia* that the absolute can be manifest in a multiplicity of incarnations, including personal lords such as Krishna and Buddha. But epistemological relativism is consistent with a moment of judgemental rationalism (in the IA). Thus the notions of *dharma* and the 'thus-formed' give an objective basis to morality (versus abstract universalising judgementalism), while the reality of free will makes it contingent whether we act morally or not.

Pythagoras tells him he is to go east to bring back the teachings of great beings, Krishna, Buddha and others. Krishna tells him his *dharma* is to synthesise East and West. He brings back to the Greek world an ethic of engaged, unattached activity in the world predicated on techniques of self-realisation. The goal of life is not to escape from the world but to be in it without attachment or aversion. Escapism is the tendential mistake of the renunciate, just as attachment or aversion is a tendential mistake of the householder. The goal of life is to love and love unconditionally – an unconditionality which transcends all fears and

4 Thus evil is an emergent product of the emergent power of free will, with emergent powers of its own.

doubts – but as realised, as *Atman*, as soul, as Self. Put another way, the goal of life is to replace or rather to implant the transcendental Self in place of the empirical ego; or, put yet another way, it is to overcome the alienation of self from Self (and thence from God and Totality). And the root cause of this alienation is *avidya* or ignorance. But *avidya* can only be overcome in practice. The techniques of self-realisation – both of action and inaction – lead to a yoga of action or phronesis, that is, practical skill in action, ultimately founded on absolute reason or cosmic consciousness and issuing in spontaneous right, maximally coherent, least-effort action. But although L2 brings back an ethic of engaged activity, he does not engage it himself. His life is an endless round (or dialectic) of travel and rest, which can only cease when the absolute is realised in the relative, in cosmic consciousness or enlightenment. However, L2's dialectic never comes to an accomplished end. There are failures of dialectics of letting go and embodiment here. He has access but cannot embody that access, because he cannot let go of a past that he has yet to clear. In L3, this will give way to a divided mind which replicates Orpheus' fate in the contradiction between lack of soul force (to be repaired in L7) and the failure to let go, specifically to forgive (to be repaired in L8).

I now want to take up the relationship between L2's thought and some other thinkers, traditions and themes. We have already seen that, opposed to Zoroastrianism and Manichaeism, evil is seen as a distortion, a dislocation, deviation from or privation of good; ultimately ignorance of alethic reality – a real but subordinated (neither co-equal nor inevitable) moment of the totality. Ultimately, it is impotent in the face of (unconditional) love, including unconditional love for oneself, which implies forgiveness and letting go of the past (the lesson L3 cannot swallow). This leads readily to the doctrine of *ahimsa* or non-violence and incorporates such practices as Pythagorean vegetarianism. On L2's travels to India, he saw the value of the doctrine of virtue as the mean in Jainism's (or so he considered) excessive and inappropriate practices, which appeared to L2 to lack discrimination in respect of objective differences within beings (for example, in regard to their possession of differential nervous systems).[5] Self-love includes of course love for one's body and integration at all levels of embodiment. This is something that L3 will never really come to terms with. In L2's dialectic of travel and rest, persistently seeking out teachers and communities, there is a curious heterocosmic affinity between the multiplicity of lovers and of teachers in this life and the variegated pantheonic multiplicity of the Upanishadic gods.

L2 finds himself very opposed to the doctrines of Kung (Confucius) and the Sophists with their stress on performance (*li*) or rhetorical success. He was much

5 He was however highly appreciative of the subtlety and caution of Jainism's epistemological relativism, in opposition to Brahmin doctrinaire dogmatism.

more sympathetic to the teachings of Anaxagoras on the ubiquity of mind, disposed (though with the important difference already noted) like the Vedics to see consciousness everywhere. He accepted Pythagoras' emphasis on structure (form) as distinct from matter. And he argued for the legitimacy, against Parmenides, of the ways of being, non-being and seeming. Non-being is not absurd but essential to being; neither is seeming absurd, and there are dialectics of correct and incorrect seeming and of being and seeming to be concerned with. In the realm of the demi-real or *avidya*, 'unity consciousness' consists in seeing how ignorance and its consequences are necessary for the full development of the concretely singularised Self overcoming or transcending its ego and its attachments; and it incorporates the conatus to do everything it can to help this process of enlightenment, everywhere in being.

It is now time to address the legacy from Laozi. For Laozi, the way is at root ineffable; or if not ineffable, something essentially to be done (and shown by example) rather than to be said, something to be grasped and practised, realised instead of (just being close) reflected upon; the reflection was only of the way insofar as it was a part of (or oriented, and intrinsically related to) the practice of its realisation. Emptiness – which connects with ineffability – is moreover the source of both heaven and earth; of the two forms that *chi* (energy) takes (*yang* and *yin*) of the five elements water, fire, wood, metal and earth and the manifest world of ten thousand things. Absence or emptiness in the form of the great void or the great ultimate (Tai Chi) both exists and is dynamic.[6] What however is the relationship between emptiness and the manifest world? Here Taoist thought takes two forms. On the first, emptiness as unboundedness, the absolute, as an absent totality, conforms to the notion of the void or unboundedness in Buddhist and Vedic texts. On the other hand, the middle truth (as promulgated and practised by L9) sees emptiness as manifest everywhere and anywhere in the flux. It puts an end to the dialectic of incessant travel by locating the great void wherever being is. (It does this however at the price of certain necessary mediations, as we shall see in Chapter 5). In any case, absence is ubiquitous; and there is no doubt that the influence of Laozi played a major part in L2's correction of Parmenides' trilemma. Other features of Laozi's thought are the injunction to act by not acting or inacting – and here we need to distinguish (a) inaction, in the sense of 'suspension of action', as in meditation from (b) inaction in the sense of spontaneous, unmediated action – the unity of microcosm and macrocosm (see heterocosmic holistic causality) and its democratic and egalitarian spirit. Tai Chi or life as a

6 Thus in Chinese, properties take a processual or verbal form. One cannot say that the grass is green but must say that the grass is greening. This is a function of the fact that there is no absolute or simple distinction between noun and verb in Chinese. Metaphysically, this reflects the fact that in their thought one thing is always passing into something else.

dynamic dance, of continual incessant movement, and of emptiness ubiquitously manifest in flux also become models of the dialectical learning process ('*karma*') involved in the cycle of birth and death.

This brings me on to the terrain of 2E; negativity and dialectic. Reincarnation was of course already accepted by Pythagoras, but the doctrine of *karma* which L2 brought over from India had its basis laid for it by the subjection of relative being by Pythagoras and Heraclitus and others to natural law. As for the associated doctrine of *moksha* or liberation, there were Orphic and Pythagorean counterparts to the practices of yoga and *yagya*. The arguments for reincarnation turn on the ubiquity (and impartiality) of ubiquity determinism; that is, of explanations for differences; the irreducibility (both causal and taxonomic) of intentional states to their physical causes, conditions or forms of manifestations, i.e. the emergence of intentionality; the unavailability of sufficient explanations for differences in intentional states in the duration of a single life; and for the unavailability of sufficient consequences for those intentional states in that life – the third feature implying pre-existence and the fourth post-existence. The ideas of reincarnation and *karma* are logical consequences of refusing both the standard alternatives of mind–body and of reason–cause dualism and reduction. That is to say, they are consequences of taking the emergence of intentional states together with their causal explicability and aefficacy seriously. Note that the endurer – or continuant, i.e. the soul – need only be a disposition to be embodied, but must be concretely singularised so that soul is to be understood as concretely singularised spirit. This adds to the argument from change to an underlying (though possibly only dispositional) continuant through change, the idea of the ingredience of spirit or God-stuff as the content of that underlying continuant. If the soul is regarded as a disposition to be embodied, then traditional Buddhist objections to a realist rendition of it are overcome. At the same time, it must be regarded as a disposition to be disembodied, i.e. liberated or free; or at least disembodied from the necessity to engage in the cycle of rebirth and redeath. This dual dispositionality of the soul to experience and to be free – to be embodied and to be disembodied – is the motor of the dialectical learning process from life to life.

What is the point about the unsettled and restless life of L2? It is fundamentally about widening experience, through the experience of change and difference, developing a conception of the relativisation and stratification of immanent being – essentially on a journey to the concrete universal – the ultimate end of the search for which is a realisation that everyone is a unique God – or, put another way, both unique and God. (And the book itself exemplifies this dialectic in a journey to this realisation, through the expression and remedying of incompleteness.) So the theme of L2 is difference and change, both phenomenologically, as experienced by L2, and theoretically, as thematised by him in his theoretical philosophy – prompted by the search for the eternal truth, a point of stability and completion.

The demarche of L2, as we have seen, is its endless accumulation, L2's failure to find and stabilise his goal (the absolute), hence its endless travel not just through lands and systems of thought but through personal relations, gurus, teachers and communities. Travel is both a metaphor for the endless round of relativity (from which liberation is sought) and the quest for the truth or the means to find liberation (which once found will require no more travelling). But L2 does experience the absolute (wholeness, totality, God, the manifestation of the dance of life) on his journey. L2 has access to the absolute but cannot embed (embody) it, because he cannot shed his past or overcome his confusions about knowledge, the goal of life and the self which also result in confusions about the character of love and the relationship between self and body (and sexuality).[7]

We can identify the sources of L2's confusions. Knowledge is practical and contextual; and the method of theoretical knowledge is dialectical or immanent–ritical. There is no unhypothetical starting point. Absolute or self is achieved as an end not experienced as a beginning from which one in daily life proceeds. There may be, as in meditation or prayer or communion, daily transcendence or access to God or one's higher self. This is indeed the daily bread, the daily subsistence and sustenance of which the New Testament speaks, but this self is always there and can be reached wherever the body or consciousness is located, just as the process of self-realisation can be carried on any of the multiplicity of paths L2 comes across.

There is confusion too about the relationship between the dialectics of shedding naturally connected with absenting (constraints – heteronomous orders of determination), which those on the path of action tend to ignore; and the dialectic of embodiment naturally connected with presenting or absenting absences, which those on the path of renunciation tend to neglect. On his journey L2 has found the 'great ultimate' time and time again, but he has not implemented it. He is too in love with the search for knowledge to realise it. While scattered and ungrounded in his community, he is too attached to his ideal and the

7 Here there is a heterocosmic affinity between his love for and accumulation of systems of theoretical knowledge and the multiplicity of loves (including types of love) and lovers in his life. Thus there is love of wisdom, love of knowledge, love of God, love of Self confused with love of self and love of body, love of man, love of woman, love of men, love of women. (Compare his adventures with *soma*, misunderstood as a missing ingredient to or as a means of extending the time available for the search for enlightenment.) Even the experience of orgasm as a 'higher state of consciousness' is misunderstood for that superconsciousness, which manifest as joy, should be a condition of daily life. By contrast *philosophia*, love of wisdom, as L9 will perceive, can be discovered as 'the great ultimate' through any path and is located, as fundamentally an ontological condition, anywhere.

quest to appreciate that he has it within his grasp. That indeed it is a condition of all his intentional acts. He is scattered...he does not find the unhypothetical starting point. He can access but not embed (embody) the self and so embeds a multiplicity of others! He is too excited to be truly focused. He is always wandering. He has secret attachments that have to be expressed and brought out in L3. L2 then has access to the absolute, but cannot embed (embody) it, because he cannot shed his past. He cannot enjoy being a man till he has come to terms with the experience of being a woman; he cannot enjoy the East until he has represented (reassimilated) the experience of the West (including, as we shall see, Atlantis). He cannot experience spiritual enlightenment until he has experienced material deprivation. If L1 was too undifferentiated and particularistic a totality, L2 has introduced principles of differentiation, change and variety. But this synthesis is too early, too quick, too soon, premature. He must learn to love himself (and himself as his Self); and so this feeling of lack of self-worth must be brought out in L3, to be transcended in practices and disciplines of loving service (in the context of a harmonious community) in L4 and then his past shed, a letting go in L5 as his fear and secret attachments are transcended in the course of an all-consuming, all-forgiving love in L5.

In sum, then, L2 sees the failure of the dialectics of shedding and embodiment; to embed the Self in the relative. This will be achieved in L8 and more especially L9. And L2 sees the failure to achieve a harmonious social existence, in an unscattered, holistically organised community. This will be achieved in L4, L10 and L11. But before he can express love and joy he must let go of bitterness; and before he can do this he must learn to trust, in a harmonious holistic community and in the context of all-forgiving and unconditional love for his Self whether by another or himself. (Eventually it will be both: in L5 we have the first, in L8 the second.)

2

PART B
UNDER THE STARS: RE-ENCHANTING REALITY

Life Three: in Ancient Greece II – the Orchard – or Orpheus in the Underworld and the perils of attachment

L2 has sown the seeds of what was already implicit in L1, namely the desire for self-realisation or enlightenment. If its greatest drawback was the failure to realise that knowledge is practical (a question of practical wisdom or phronesis), contextual, processual and immanent–critical (rather than inductive or deductive–accumulative or foundationalist), it nevertheless solidly established and exemplified the relativisation and stratification of immanent being. L2 then is a life in which ontological access is not embedded (in a dialectic of embodiment) in the relative field. L2 is characterised by karmic residues from the past, excess baggage constituting so much unnecessary entourage which must be brought into the open and cleared in L3. But L3 cannot completely let go, she cannot completely come to love and accept herself, as thus-formed, and let go of her past. In it she does, however, express a desire for unity with and indeed an identification with the oppressed and suffering; in particular, in what I have been calling structural sin, the collective (or more generally social structural) variant of personal or argentive evil. This identification with the oppressed sets up the seeds of the desire not just for individual but for universal self-realisation, which is to become an increasing motif of the odyssey of the soul, especially from L11 on. This can only be achieved in a dialectical universalisation of the sort of practices and communities in which the soul will engage in L4 and to a degree elsewhere (for example, in L10 and L11) later on. But let me now turn to the bare bones of L3, which is a bookish and isolated one. (In L4 the soul will be bookish too, but as a writer as well as a reader and in the context of a practically oriented community.)

In L3 the soul is again reincarnated in Ancient Greece, but this time as a woman. Her father, the aged head of a powerful and learned family (is he in fact none other than the metamorphosised L2? I leave this matter aside for the moment), like her otherwise childless mother, had wanted a boy. And this is the *karma* to be worked out in this life: to be a woman in a male-dominated world. A very pure spirit, she herself wonders at an early age why this is so – that is, why is she a girl? – and why the world is male-dominated. Clear and serious in disposition, taking joy in nature and learning, she has at a young age psychic dreams (or are they really visions?) of an early Atlantean age – of which she had, or was to come to possess, some knowledge from Orphic, Pythagorean and Platonic texts – when women, and especially priestesses, were dominant. She appears to herself in a flashback – in a flashback of a flashback in the philosopher's (L14's) time machine (is this flashback in the Ancient Greek's or in the French philosopher's?) – as just such a priestess, practitioner of the occult arts and guardian and gardener of the mysteries. Here and now she is somewhat obsessed by water, both to drink and to wash, as if feeling the need to continually atone for and purify herself for sins (real or imagined) she had committed in the past. Thus later in life she has a vision in which she sees herself abusing – or sexually maltreating – and otherwise draining her father and her uncle in Atlantean times; the very father and his brother who abuse her now.

Let us take the question of power and abuse of power. Innocently breaking a pot – an earthenware water jug, scattered into so many pieces (*déjà vu*) – she is beaten by her father, in marked contradistinction to the experience of L1. Taking, accused of stealing (attachment to possessions is another theme which is raised crucially by this life, implicating as it does the agent in object referral rather than subject–referral and tying the agent to reincarnation in the relative field of existence), an apple from her uncle's orchard, she is beaten by her uncle, who threatens to tell her father, unless she consents to continue this practice (from which he derives sadistic sexual satisfaction) on a regular basis. Paradoxically, she feels as once both rejected and relieved when he stops this process. Masochism, narcissism and a combination of a longing for the past and a yearning for an unperceived future are secret motifs of this life.

If L2 is a drifter, L3 is a dreamer. This life is also noticeable for (1) the priority in the Orphic as distinct from say the oral traditions of India, of the written over the oral, of writing and reading over speaking, generally her bookishness; (2) emphasis and symbolic attention on the prohibited and the oppressed; (3) once more, as in L2, problems in relation to community and family; and (4) what we may characterise as negative excess, a self-induced deficiency of food and other earthly necessities and/or pleasures. The real sub-texts of this life are Orpheus and Atlantis. In her visions of Atlantis she sees herself as an Atlantian princess with a glittering diamond on her brow. In this life we (or rather L14 in his time machine) see a symbol of purity and *kundalini* energy rise like fire from her crown *chakra*. We also see her in a circle of fellow culties. And in the background there is a flowing purifying cross, signifying that the Christ energy – to be most manifest in L5 – will purify, atone and forgive transgressions of power (free will manifest as sin – structural and personal or agentive). The real question is will she forgive and unconditionally love herself, accepting herself as thus-formed, letting go of the past and hence any need for further atonement or suffering on its account, freeing herself for her new incipient vocation or *dharma* to be an agent of universal self-realisation or emancipation, including emancipation from all abuses of power and structurally or otherwise engendered forms of oppression. This goal becomes easier to see achievable in perspective when we realise that the totality of master–slave relationships depends essentially on the creativity of the slaves; and in contemporary capitalism on both a rising organic composition of ideas (and hence upon so to speak the transcendent) and a rising organic composition of nature, generating contradictions at both poles.

At any rate, after the early episodes of sexual abuse, she is betrothed at the age of sixteen (by which time she is already beginning to starve and otherwise deprive herself, becoming too thin to be an object of sexual attraction for her uncle, as well as too old and wise). She is betrothed into a family of similar caste. But as the menfolk are away at war (as L2's father had intended for *him*), she seldom sees her fiancé and husband-to-be and instead busies herself with practical, especially educational, affairs. Thus, fully literate, she takes on responsibility for educating and otherwise caring for (we see her busily shopping in a bustling bazaar and leading an outwardly active life[1]) the young, although she is to remain childless (and indeed effectively celibate) herself. (The menfolk are the absent presences in her life.) Although obsessed by bodily purification she is, like L2, a busy bee. At any rate she shares the interests of her predecessor in L2[2] (though not perhaps at a superficial level its interest); 'there is little to say; the men are away', is her ironic reflection on her society. She becomes a member of a secret Orphic cult whose symbol is the apple. Half muse, half oracle, she spends much time practising secret rites, meditating, contemplating and reading especially in her uncle's favourite orchard grove, now bequeathed to her by her father upon his brother's death. She practises an extreme form of Pythagorean vegetarianism, eating only fruit, especially lemons and oranges. She fasts frequently and is concerned to cleanse and purify the physical vehicle (which she however neglects to sufficiently nourish), practising taking the energy upwards, towards, into and out of her crown *chakra*. This is the dialectic of the snake-like *kundalini* energy. The apple, redolent of the Garden of Eden story, symbolises intentionality, while its theft symbolises the abuse of power from Atlantian times; or so at least it can be

1 It is inwardly active too; she is a contemplative *yoghini* and voracious reader of Orphic and other esoteric philosophical and political texts.

2 She even sings Orphic renditions of Vedic hymns brought back by him from India.

conjectured. Obsessed by bodily purification (occasionally chastising it, while continually cleansing and otherwise purifying it), she cannot complete the dialectic of shedding by letting go of her (contrition for her real or imagined) past and letting go of her bitterness and resentment about her present situation. Eventually she dies at an early age of malnutrition, choking on an olive in her last breath. She has however been a strong woman and her dream of equality with men, if not the superiority that women and especially priestesses achieved in Atlantean times – where she was especially adept in the use of crystals and at astral travel – sets up a yearning for balance between male and female aspects, and more generally for the reconciliation and resynthesis of Pythagorean dyads and heterocosmically related opposites – such as absolute and relative, east and west, male and female, reason and experience, mind and body, *yin* and *yang*, action and inaction, presence and absence, positive and negative, heaven and earth – which can only be achieved in a forthcoming age of enlightenment.

Outwardly, L3 is active but uneventful. Much of her time is spent waiting for the menfolk to return from war. Waiting, she forms friendships with male slaves – especially one from Egypt (the Arab tradesman, the father of her love in L2, who took advantage of her and betrayed her into a den of thieves in what is now Baghdad) and a Jew from Palestine (who she will renew acquaintance with in L4) – initiating them into the Orphic mysteries. Her passions are music, singing, poetry and reading; meditating; fasting and cleansing (though not outwardly obsessed with possessions, she is somewhat obsessed with excretion – the feeling: to produce, to be poetic) and she also writes a little. She is above all however a bookish reader, a cultivator and educator, a *yoghini* in waiting. It is, however, not or not only a husband[3] which she needs, but unconditional love and forgiveness for herself. Only this will allow her to be in the moment of her being, to live in the present.

L3, like L8, shows the suppression and suffering, but also the strength of womankind. She shows patience and fortitude and to an extent overcomes envy and bitterness (as in sour fruits). She readily forgives and gives (though not perhaps as readily as L8), but the one she will not forgive is herself or let go of her attachment to the past. Is she a member of a cult springing up in the wake of or currently informed by L2? Or is she in fact the autogenetic self-production of

3 I say 'not only' bearing in mind that there is a dialectic of inner and outer fulfilment, of absolute and relative (including objectively constituted demi-real) being. It is of course objectively and subjectively constituted demi-real being which it is the object of the process of self-realisation to transform. I am taking it as understood that the basis of objectively constituted demi-real being is the subjectivity of the agents who reproduce it. When I refer to subjectively constituted being, I am here talking about mere semblance or seeming, the sense in which the world of *maya* also contains more or less subjective or idiosyncratic illusions and delusions.

L2, a result of a somatic implosion, or transformation of one polar opposite into its other, an old man into a young woman? Leaving this aside, let us reiterate that lack of opportunity to and suppression of women, and the abuse of power (in what I have called master–slave relationships generally) and even more generally suffering as such, are (or can be) examples of *structural sin* and derive from the autonomy of emergent laws, i.e. in the human world the dialectic of pre-existing structure and free will. So within the re-enchanted reality of the ancient Greek lives of Chapter 2 of this narrative (and the dialectic of absolute and relative reality in geo-history) are inscribed all the evils of demi-reality, ultimately products of *avidya* and attachment (on which more anon). Purity is a dominant motif in L3, to be resumed in L4. But there community is found. Social alienation is overcome, though the path followed is still essentially that of the renunciate. L4 is also about treading the middle path, the two vices for every virtue and in particular the vice or excess of under-nourishment (of body, mind and spirit).

There are some further points to be made about L3:

(1) L3 is above all about collective, as well as individual, *karma* and especially the *karma* of women, of Atlantis, and of women in Atlantis. We shall see this again in a more microscopic context in L13, who picks up on the Italian *karma* partly incurred by L6 (and other Italian lives); or L11, who must engage with the Indian *karma* incurred in several lives preceding it (especially lives between L5 and L6). But L3 is not only about collective *karma*; it is also about the fate of world civilisations. Thus there are unsettling parallels, as well as particular differentiations, between Atlantean civilisation at the time of its demise and contemporary global capitalist, more generally Western, civilisation: genetic engineering, abuse of astral (as distinct from merely physical) technology,[4] exploitation (the abuse of $power_1$ in $power_2$ or master–slave relationships) and ecological contradiction were all rife.[5]

(2) In a way, L3 recapitulates the fate of Orpheus. There is a contradiction between (a) soul force and (b) practice (the failure to let go of the presence of the past) manifesting a contradiction between the sublime and the quotidian. This contradiction, indicating a divided mind, is further exasperated in L7, where the inner anger of L3 explodes into the outer anger of L7. There however it is also at least partly assuaged and takes the more constructive form of the development of the will. (Anger is always an expression of inner conflict.) The failure to let go and forgive is overcome by the practices of loving service in L4 and above all by the unconditional love and forgiveness the soul receives and in turn expresses in

4 Though as the astral contains the physical, this also has its physical effects.

5 See the two contradictions of the capitalist mode of production already indicated above, namely (1) a rising organic composition of ideas and (2) a rising organic composition of nature.

L5. This theme of loving service and of a perhaps too immediate realisation of the absolute in the relative, as we shall see, is continued in the lives of service and love of L8 and L9. The exploding anger of L7 expressing the inner conflict and divided mind of L3 (to be manifest in a different form in L6), is mollified and controlled in the mindful expression of the will in the focused activity of L8 and L9, further accentuated by the practices of meditation and mindfulness in terms of which so much of L10 and L11 is formed.

This contradiction between (a) and (b) is of course a stigma of the failure of the dialectic of embedding the absolute in the relative and is manifest in all kinds of theory/practice contradictions and splits and contradictions. These block activity and prohibit being-in-the-moment; that action without blockage or drainage, which depends upon attention to the present and intention for the future, which necessitates that lightness or freedom from excess baggage, the accumulated inheritance of the past, prohibiting what could be called – in virtue of its immediacy, directness, spontaneity and correctness – straight-through or straight-away action, that spontaneous right action or negentropic action, reversing entropy, action without blockage or drainage, which is least effort and least energy dissipating, maximally coherent (and aefficacious), creative and compassionate. This depends upon accepting each moment as thus-formed (as not now undoable), as perfect (understood in the totality of circumstances and determinations that produced it and in the totality of opportunities it affords). Understanding and accepting each moment as in itself perfect makes it perfect, and such acceptance is also a precondition for change; that is, for making the next moment even more perfect than the previous one. So L3, like Orpheus, betrays the present (and hence the future) for the past, carrying too much excess baggage, insufficiently light (insufficiently en-lightened) and fails to complete the dialectic of shedding (the past, heteronomous orders of determination, accumulated entropy, constraints, ingrained habitual constraining dispositions, based on *avidya* or ignorance understood as practical) and more generally the dialectic of individual self-realisation. Its focus on collective *karma* and structural sin, however, lays the agenda for the programme of universal self-realisation to be increasingly of concern in the developing trajectory of the soul. This is the real gain of L3.

(3) Masochism. This can be conceived in three main ways. The first is as an attempt to focus on or an identification with the oppressed, prohibited (censored), underside, devalued member of Pythagorean dyads or heterocosmic couples or polar opposites or its symbols or martyrs, harbingers or saints. In this respect, masochism has an affinity with Zen and tantric practices of using prohibited or bizarre or taboo modes of behaviour as a means of expressing deep or profound spiritual truths; in rather the same way as I have argued (in *PON* C2.5)

social crises can express deep truths about social structural reality.[6] Second, it may also be a way of focusing on or discharging the burden of individual or collective *karma*,[7] particularly when introjected as guilt or shame. Third, it also signifies holding on, refusal to love self (unconditionally) or sadism-to-self, just as sadism signifies a refusal to love others unconditionally, more precisely it is self-hatred projected onto others.[8] Here again one is involved in dialectics of the mean, of the journey to the equilibrium or balance point from which point alone dharmic action is possible.

(4) Possessiveness. Failure to let go is a form of attachment, and L3 illustrates the perils of attachment to the past. In this case the past is something one (still) *has*, rather than being merely something that has happened to one, and that, as such, has *passed*, is over, has gone. We have seen that the philosophy of self-realisation, including its inexorable corollary universal self-realisation, depends on a subject-referential rather than object-referential attitude or outlook to life. This is the true basis of the prohibition on theft. What you can't find in yourself you can't nick from another. However, the very institution of property presupposes the absence of trust, the absence of a society based on and expressing total unconditional love. Money is the dominant means by which energy circulates in a society based on attachment and aversion. It cannot, however, substitute for the energy which cosmic consciousness or enlightenment affords. The feeling that it can was of course behind the practice of the sale of indulgences that L6 (secretely) deplored and the attempts made over and over again to try to buy salvation by so many (exemplified in this book by L7 and L12).

(5) Narcissism. I will discuss the whole topic of identification and sexual ambiguity in the context of L12. Here it is sufficient to note that narcissism in the sense of true love for oneSelf, as distinct from mere love for oneself or even merer love for one's body, is the real basis of all altruism. True Self love is at one with love for God and carries with it a conatus to love for all other Selves, as concretely singularised and manifest in the context of particular relationships in which love, including sexual love, for the other (or indeed same) sex has its natural place.

(6) The mean and excess. L6 illustrates the failure to get the dialectic of inner and outer fulfilment, of absolute and relative well-being on the journey to self-realisation right. It illustrates the vice of privation or negative excess. This has a cosmic significance in that lack or incompleteness is behind all excess, imbalance and lack of integration (both of positive and negative types) based as they are

6 This refers to the whole theme of the primacy of the pathological.

7 Collective *karma* can hold at any or for any aspect of community; for example, there can be familial, regional, occupational, national (etc.) *karmas*.

8 This does not mean that mild pain cannot be pleasurable.

alike on forms of *avidya*. The non-avidyaic act of getting it right, the knack of getting things exactly right,[9] is a spontaneous act of creativity from a transcendent cause on to an immanent ground already prepared for by the practice of the agent (or agents) concerned. Life is a learning or teaching (tutorial) situation. There are three important aspects to this. The first is avoiding judgementalism. Hegel was very wise to see that 'I' indexes both someone unique, someone in particular and everyone and anyone at all (and does so in the same particular way). Thus, for example, this story is not about an ego. We have all been rich and poor, male and female, oppressor and oppressed, and so on. Anyone can play any role in the holistic performance which is life, and a particular life in a particular Life (such as L3) in the odyssey of some particular, concretely singularised soul. This is the standpoint of unity consciousness: to learn from all and to see God (or the absolute) in all; the first is more precisely the level of 'God-consciousness,' seeing the highest relative value in all, which unity consciousness both presupposes and transcends. Second, acceptance of a personal situation as 'thus-formed' does not militate against attempts to transform that situation in the future. Rather, attention to the present and acceptance of it as always already formed, however it has been (a function of the irreversibility of tensed time), is a necessary condition for its intentional transformation, beginning as it always (and only ever) does now in and for the present-future. Nor does it tell against the attempts to construct parallel and multiple universes (exemplified by L2's alternative histories of the ending of his life), based on alternative constructions as to what might have been grounded in the actualisation of alternative sets of powers or alternative actualisations of the same set of powers, as a propadeutic to consideration as to how to change – for all action is inevitably change or transformation – the world for the better in the future. Acceptance of the present situation as 'thus-formed' (and thus formed in part by the exercises of our free will) is a necessary condition for its transformation by intentional action (or exercises of our free will) in the present-future.

(7) Finally, we should note that both L2 and L3 re-emphasise the value of Buddha's understanding and stress on the fact, causes and cure of suffering (and its overcoming in enlightenment) as to do with essentially *practical* affairs. This is the value of the notion of *avidya* as practical. Both L2 and L3 live lives which are replete with theory–practice contradictions. In particular, they fail to embed the absolute in relative reality despite their varied experiences of the absolute and their (different) commitments to this project. Their lives illustrate how dicey is the dialectic of absolute and relative, of inner and outer well-being. They both illustrate a failure in the dialectics of shedding and embodiment to the point

9 The Vedic 'siddhi' (or perfection).

where action from a standpoint in which the absolute is embedded in the relative, namely spontaneous right action, or what I called 'straight-through' or 'straight-away' action, action without the entropic inertia of the past, is possible. Spontaneous right action is action which is once totally free, in expressing the nature of the self as concretely singularised and thus-formed spirit, and maximally right (coherent, aefficacious and so on). Action from this standpoint is radically free and sufficient to obtain its ends, no longer necessitated or bound by the dictates of quantum natural law or *karma* or the presence and aefficacy of the past. Straight-away, straight-through, basic-like, spontaneous right action is also the most *creative* (coming *ex nihilo*, unmediated by thought processes) and forms a component or aspect of every genuinely transformative human act. In this way, the essential creativity and freedom of men and women sustain the totality of master–slave relationships and the suffering, oppression and so on that characterise the relative demi-real world of *avidya*. And in this fact lies the eternal possibility and condition of a true and universal enlightenment, the embedding of the absolute in the relative, not just in individual self-realisation but in that form of universal self-realisation which I have called 'unity existence'.[10]

10 In the conception of life as a learning or teaching situation the concept of master–pupil relations, based on recognition of the fundamental essential unity and equality of mankind together with the specific differentiations and concrete singularities of the *dharma* of particular individuals and the *karma* imposed upon them, replaces the notion of master–slave relations, i.e. relations of exploitation or oppression based on the abuse of power. Master–pupil relationships recognise the craft character of knowledge, while the reification and alienation inherent in master–slave relationships suppress the creativity and freedom involved in every genuinely transformative human act as well as buttressing an alienated and reifying account of knowledge. Moreover the teaching situation is holistic. All master–pupil relationships are an abstraction from a totality in which each and all learn from everything. Thus the master learns from the pupil; and all become masters and pupils in turn. This does not abolish but universalises essentially unilateral, progressive development.

INTERLUDE

From East To West: retrospect and prospect – sketches

1 The fundamental failure of L2 then is ignorance over the nature of ignorance. The fundamental failure of L3 is lack of unconditional love and forgiveness for herself, manifest in the form of attachment to, failure to let go of, the past.

L2 has no appreciation of knowledge (including the overcoming of *avidya*, the root of all ill), as *practical*. This involves seeing it is as *inter alia* an intuitive and a heart affair, as well as developing, incomplete and open-ended; as step-at-a-time, contextual, immanent and so on; holistic; situational; processual; a matter of degree; as a skill, capacity, disposition; as in-the-moment; as *ex nihilo*. *Inter alia*, this will overcome the false subjectively centred, objectively constituted layers of illusion constituting *maya*: beliefs, informing wants, desires and fears and heteronomous orders of determination (so much excess, unnecessary, baggage). This is partly corrected by mindfulness and meditation in L10 and the practical experiences of L12 to L15.[1] L2 has a defective understanding of totality; more generally of the triple-pronged goal of life (on which more in a moment; see 2

1 One of the innovations of this book is a new theory – or rather a development of the existing dialectical critical realist – theory of knowledge; of *avidya* or ignorance (in particular the failure to practically realise our own essential and real, though occluded, enlightenment) as the cause of all ill; and of liberation. Note that if reincarnation and *karma* turn on emergence, liberation depends on 'disemergence'. L2 sees emergence as underpinning both reincarnation and *karma* and evil, and disemergence as underpinning liberation. This results in spontaneous right action, which may be defined as optimum or best action (including nature support), that is, the action which, in the totality of circumstances and determinations which actually prevail, produces the best, most aefficacious (correct or right) result (therefore most place-timely and so on). The desideratum is of course intentionality (emergence) without attachment (to be disemerged), as in the role of the will (developed in L7) and discipline and service (developed in L4 and L8). One gain of L2 is the resolution of the problem of evil, at least formally in dialectics of inaction. Thus the reality (emergence) and irreality (including its dependence, as error, on deficiency or lack) of evil appears as a warp, which however he does not shed so that in practice it holds him (L2) back as so much excess baggage. A corresponding gain of L14 is the resolution of the problem of structural sin (which undergirded L3's dilemmas and contradictions) in dialectics of action. In both cases the form is seen as 'warped', that is as both real and illusory, that is, as though emergent, also dependent upon *maya* and *avidya* (and hence lack).

below). He is carrying so much excess baggage, which stems from ontological insecurity (alienation from Self), inducing inner split and a lack of trust, and generates the failure to stabilise and integrate the techniques of self-realisation he has laboriously compiled and theoretically understood (without practically realising), and ultimately leads to the delusory search for *soma*. L3 also has excess baggage (the dialectic of heteronomous determinations), particularly in the form of the failure to forgive (looking back) and let go, to accept (as thus-formed) and trust God (i.e. including her true Self). L2 isolates the dialectic of shedding (on which more in (3) below) but does not shed, instead accumulating. L3 is caught in a contradiction between the sublime and the quotidian, the absolute and the relative, between soul force[2] and attachment (understood as involving all levels), manifest in the failure to let go. This is also manifest as a contradiction between *dharma* and *karma*; between God and the presence of the past, excess baggage, ingrained habits, dispositions (beliefs) informing wants, desires, fears, and other emotional states involving attachment or aversion. This becomes the divided minds of L6 and L14 (divided, that is, between spirituality and intellectuality) and is expressed in L7 in the manifestation or eruption of the inner anger (self-hatred, anger and loathing, guilt and shame) of L3 into the outer anger, violence and hatred of L7. The necessary shedding is partly achieved by lives of service in L4 and L5 (particularly L5, which recapitulates the experience of Jesus' own life and in which Jesus, in completely opening L5's heart *chakra*, in a manifestation of total unconditional love and forgiveness, enables L5 to transcend his fears and lack of trust and so on his return to Palestine carry on his work without fear, doubt or trepidation) and L8 and L9. L9 is of course the life of enlightenment-in-alienation, and it motivates the project of universal self-realisation in L10 and L11 to overcome social, including religious and communal splits, dichotomies and alienations; to go West, and to go basic (therefore the process of self-realisation or enlightenment or the transcending or overcoming of *avidya* is to become fully embodied and integrated and consequently involve complete purification and shedding in L15); to concretise[3] and dialectically universalise and moreover universally accessibilise; to understand socio-economic/political and other structural (including global ecological) determinations. In L2, the problem of evil is resolved as involving the co-presence of autonomous and heteronomous determinations, as dependent upon emergence and 'free will'. In L14, the problem of structural sin is formulated, and its resolution is seen to require collective and totalising agency, including the dialectic of desire to freedom to universal

2 Soul force may be defined as the degree of the soul's access to and integration and embodiment (including aefficacy – i.e. realisation) in the life and activity of the person.

3 As L10 and L11 realised, compassion implies acceptance and recognition of difference, and of the social totality as a unity-in-diversity; in effect as a concrete universal.

self-realisation in the drive to what I have called 'unity existence'. In short, L2 knows but does not practise.

2 The goal of life is:

(1) The full development of the concretely singularised, individuated, soul as thus-formed;
(2) To learn to experience (give and receive) unconditional love (and forgiveness);

and

(3) to realise its essential God nature.

(1) and (2) depend upon the process of learning (and we are throughout conceiving life as a learning, teaching situation) action (including referential detachment) without attachment. (3) depends on dialectics of self-realisation. Self-realisation is a process, a matter of degree and a practical affair. (Thus L2 knows_t but does not practise (know_p) these techniques.) As we have seen, dialectics of shedding do not exhaust dialectics of inaction. For, for example, a soul may be pure but not have penetrated all aspects of the reality it has chosen to engage with. (1)–(3) presuppose overcoming *avidya* – i.e. enlightenment – as a matter of increasing degree, process, practical realisation. (1) and (2) presuppose the development of cosmic consciousness to unity consciousness, so that we can understand the reason why, as thus-formed, the soul has had to encounter the aspects or levels of reality (including wrong, evil, error) dependent on but irreducible to lack (epistemically immanent incompleteness) that it must relinquish and let go of, displace, replace by God. At the level of unity consciousness, ultimately the demi-real level is seen as unnecessary necessity; necessary for the experience of the relative world and development of the soul, but unnecessary in that it is ultimately overcome in one or more dialectics of inaction or action. At this point I want to say a bit more about fear and desire. Fear is just desire to avoid the situation feared. Desire is just fear of not possessing the object, situation and so on which is desired. So we have the theorem of the mutual implication of fear and desire. Moreover both are grounded in ontological insecurity, i.e. alienation of self from Self, i.e. lack of integration or totality. The path of development just is the dialectic to greater totality, through transcendence of splits, alienations, conflicts and so on, ultimately to self-determination = liberation = totality. Both fear and desire moreover are based on beliefs, and beliefs are to be analysed as more or less ingrained, habitual dispositions. The false beliefs which inform fears and desires are based on *avidya* or ignorance of the true nature of things (including especially the Self). All dialectics of action and inaction ultimately lead

to enlightenment. But there is a practical distinction to be made between the dialectics of shedding and embodiment. Purity is freedom from heteronomous determination, which is the same thing as self-determination; and the dialectic of purification is a dialectic of disemergence, of shedding, of liberation.

3 I now want to say a bit more about the dialectic of shedding, particularly in the context of the dialectic of co-presence and the theme of absence.

(i) In the context of the dialectic (co-presence) of autonomous (realist) and heteronomous (irrealist) determinations, liberation must be conceived as the *shedding* (letting go) of heteronomous orders of determination. (However the dialectic of shedding is not the same as the dialectic of embodiment, which consists in infusing spirit into the experience of all necessary levels of being for a particular form of life. Total purification is however equivalent to self-determination.) This is equivalent to unveiling = removal of ignorance, understood as (a) practical, (b) informing (error/evil depends upon lack), as false beliefs, fears and desires[4] and (3) the root of all ills. Error is here seen as the co-presence of real emergence and illusion (ignorance, absence). The result is as we have seen in the appendix to Chapter Two Part A a *stratified* monism; real illusion, evil, structural sin exists.

(ii) Man is essentially (d_r) free, but this freedom is not realised (d_a) or experienced (d_e); essentially one, but concretely singularised and thus-formed (and in particular formed in different (combinations of) traditions); and essentially Godlike = full of love/unbounded in potential (power). So we have the theorem of the essential unity of man as Godly. The goal of life is to realise man's concretely singularised divinity; and in particular, through experience of the emotions as signalling devices on earth, to live a life in and of unconditional love.

(iii) The mechanism of human bondage is *avidya*; error, informing evil, structural sin, and, as beliefs, underpinning desires and fears, particularly in the form of lack of knowledge of Self, or alienation of self from Self. *Avidya* is understood as real emergent illusion and so therefore as dependent upon lack or absence.

(iv) Absence appears, as emptiness, beyond, between, the unbounded (the unknown, the unexperienced and so on), the void, or just simply incompleteness, as the fundamental ontological category necessary for change and being. Thus we have the dialectical nature of the self as both (2E) in development – life as Tai Chi; and (3L) in interconnection – life as heterocosmic community. Normatively negative absence is epistemically immanent, normatively positive absence epistemically transcendent; in the former guise it appears as incompleteness generating inconsistency and split; in the latter form as the source of all creativity *ex nihilo*, as a transcendent cause on to an immanent ground.

4 It follows from this that lack of unconditional love is a category mistake.

Human bondage is characterised by *avidya*, *maya*, attachment and object referral; the desire to have, rather than to be (subject referral); the confusion of Self with possessions, money and so on; the failure to let go (the blocking of God-nature, *dharma*, soul force and spontaneous right action by heteronomous orders of determination and constraint, *karma*, excess baggage, and so on); and confusion over identity as such including self-identity, sexual identity and ambivalence over self, love, God and so on.

(v) The mechanism of human liberation is above all the dialectic of desire for freedom ((a) for individual liberation, and (b) for universal self-realisation or unity existence through a dialectic involving the growth of compassion, Godliness, love and unity consciousness). This occurs through the self-undermining, insistent and repetitive (badly infinite in Hegelian terms) character of desire and fear; and the character of life as a teaching situation, evolving through as a learning process of reincarnation, *karma*, liberation eventually leading to universal self-realisation.[5] The transcendental deduction of reincarnation and *karma* turns on the irreducibility of intentional states; the ubiquity (of ubiquity) determinism; and the unavailability of sufficient causes (implying pre-existence) or consequences (implying post-existence) for intentional components of actions in the life in which they occur. Specifically, the dialectics of self-realisation are dialectics of inaction: (1) of access; (2) of shedding (purification, clearing, letting go, elimination and so on); (3) embodiment (integration); and (4) witnessing-in-activity. And dialectics of action are specifically (5) of praxis; (6) the dialectic of desire for freedom proper through collective and totalising agency including socio-economic/political and ecological action; (7) compassion (what is one's is, through God, each and all's); and (8) philosophical recapitulation or recollection.

(vi) All change begins with self-change, and even the slightest act of self-observation begins to change the world.

4 L2 accumulates knowledge but misunderstands the nature of misunderstanding. L3 purifies the bodily vehicle (and her mind to an extent) but not her heart; she cannot forgive herself. It is fear which underpins this failure to let go, to trust. Expansion and embodiment will occur in L4, but the fear is only overcome in L5. However, elements of the contradiction of L3 are still left after L5, in the divided minds of L6 and L7, only to be overcome by the lives of service and

5 As I have already indicated in this teaching situation, the concept of master–pupil relations comes to the fore and replaces that of master–slave relations. Master–pupil relations are non-exploitative, non-abusive and consistent with equality, mutual recognition (based on appreciation of the concrete singularity of the individuals involved) and friendship. They are founded on a craft and practically oriented view of knowledge. And hence to the removal of *avidya* as a practical affair, as I have been stressing, and to the realisation of enlightenment as en-lightenment, the shedding of illusions constituting so much excess (unnecessary) baggage.

enlightenment in L8 and L9 respectively. The lesson of mindfulness and being in the moment and the stabilisation of techniques of self-realisation are gradually installed in L10 and L11 in the formulation of the project of universal self-realisation. This is necessary to overcome the social alienation (experienced even in the enlightenments of L9 to L11) and can only be achieved after full embodiment and saturation in the socio-economic-political world in L11 to L15.

Let me sum up, at this intermediate stage, the basic thesis of this book. Man is essentially *free*; and essentially *God*. Therefore Man is essentially *one*, but as a unity-in-diversity, that is as concretely singularised, and is therefore also essentially *unique*. Man is essentially *creative*. Man is essentially *being* (subject-referential) rather than *having* (attached, object-referential); and this being is to be embodied, in intentional engaged but unattached activity. Man is essentially *enlightened*, not ignorant (avidyic). The totality of master–slave relationships, including internalised ones, depends entirely on the creativity of slaves and in this consideration lies the possibility, rather inexorability, of their emancipation. Similarly, evil is entirely parasitic on good, and the very possibility of attachment depends upon the separation and autonomy of being from having. Action is naturally dharmic, spontaneously right, and *karma* is literally a thing of the past. Spontaneously, action is spontaneously right; it is heteronomous mediations that make it erroneous evil or otherwise wrong. The dialectic of emancipation is essentially one of disemergence, in which the emergence of intentionality, freedom and creativity is preserved at the expense of the rejection of unnecessary and injurious heteronomous orders of constraint and determination. To be free, we only have to become what we essentially are.

3

ON THE PATH: OR TO THE PROMISED LAND PART II

Life Four: Scrolling – the Writer

I will be brief with the two lives, L4 and L5, to be discussed in this chapter as they form the subject of a future, much fuller, study.

In L4 we see the soul as a scribe in the Essene headquarters at Qumran by the Dead Sea, busily at work with some others on the texts which have become known as the Dead Sea Scrolls. He is at one with the angelic forces of night and day, and he shares the lifestyles and beliefs of his Essene brothers and sisters. This is a happy and long life, spent in harmony with nature and his fellow human beings. If L1 establishes its vocation as a teacher and L2 as a philosopher, the soul has by now, in this and L2 and the bookish L3, found its vocation as a writer. Unlike L2 and L3, however, the soul (understood as concretely singularised, individuated, spirit (God-stuff)) has at last satisfied its desire for an integrated harmonious community. This is a life without alienation from community, though there are forebodings of the impending alienations *of* the community. This is a life of rest and peace; of love and joy and service; of discipline and harmony; of satisfactory master/pupil relations, in which the practical roots of *avidya* or ignorance are gnawed away at and real access, shedding, embodiment and witnessing, real focused activity, real mindfulness, real being in the moment, real balance in the totality of activities of life is achieved.

So L4 leads a long and happy, almost idyllic existence; productive and pure in thought, word and deed. Born in Jericho, his spiritual potential is seen and he joins the Essene settlement in Qumran, after the elders have patiently negotiated with and persuaded his parents to let go of him. (This is a motif which will recur in the story in different ways: thus the father who gives the child away in Tibet in L10 becomes the grieving mother in L11; and the Tibetan mother becomes the Indian father concerned now for his son's spiritual development.) He is taken for training to Karmel and spends many months, totalling some year or two, there as well as being schooled in Qumran. He undergoes various initiations, eventually becoming one of the elders of the community himself. He spends much time in the scriptorium, writing with a younger man (AC) who will become his love in his Chinese female life (L8). Everything must be written in duplicate, as if in foreboding of the tribulations and assaults to come. Eventually he becomes a spiritual teacher and moves on from the communal settlement to live up in the caves. He inhabits a cave close to the one he did in L1, coming down periodically to teach or to go on trips to Karmel, Jerusalem or other centres. One of his pupils becomes his teacher in his next life (L5); both will remember this. His psychic and intuitive powers develop. He learns to travel astrally. He lives to be very old. As a child he breaks a chalice; he pieces together the chalice and keeps it as a continual reminder of the transience of all terrestrial (including symbolic) things.

The lesson of L4 is that a life of service is not at odds with self-realisation;[1] nor (to an extent in contrast with L3) need it be unhappy; or one of alienation from the community. Like L3, L4 is bookish, but at last the desire for an integrated harmonious community existence is satisfied; there is no alienation from the community (although there are premonitions of alienation of the community) and it is a life of peace in which the quest implicit in the dialectic of absolute and relative finds a temporary equilibrium point or point of rest, of ontological retreat which is a real flourishing of the absolute in a community dedicated to the absolute and its realisation in the relative round of existence.

In this community each morning and evening, at least while he is at the main site in Qumran, he takes the morning and evening Essene communions. Each morning is dedicated to an angel associated with the Earthly Mother. From Sunday through to Saturday respectively, these are the angels of earth, life, joy, the sun, water, air and the Earthly Mother Herself. Each evening is dedicated to an angel associated with the Heavenly Father. From Sunday through to Saturday, these are those of creative work, peace, power, love, wisdom, the Heavenly Father Himself and eternal life. One Sunday evening he feels a great force descend upon his head, at his crown *chakra*, experiencing it visibly expanding, and sensing within him the very presence and being of the angel of creative work. He is to be the bumble bee, the creative worker, the transformer who pollinates the roses (and other flowers) of enlightenment. This is the soul's vocation, its *dharma*. He recognises it then and attempts to realise it in practice in this life and the others to come. But in addition, each day he will try to apply the principle of the angelic force or essence of that day. Thus on Tuesdays he will try to express joy in everything, on Wednesdays love, and so on.

The French philosopher L14 who is observing all this is fascinated with his developing psychic powers. He has himself tried to photograph, as we have

1 Compare the Vedic, 'I am the Totality'.

already noticed, angels and fairies. He is quite prepared to see the development of clairvoyant powers as the opening up of natural intrinsic powers inherent (already inherent) in actually existing mankind, as part of the unfinished (including perceptual) evolution of the species. He observes L4 tutoring novices in their development, teaching the novices to see space as filled, beginning by focusing on and around the borders, boundaries, edges of things and advising them not to be afraid of the creative imagination, which is but the veil to reality. L14 is likewise fascinated by his developing powers of astral travel (also a throwback to the life observed or imagined by L3 of Atlantian times). He notices that the astral world contains and is as real as everything in the physical world, but that it too does not exhaust reality itself. At the astral and the higher levels of vibration, everything physical takes on a more malleable and dreamlike character. But it does not lose its sensuality or solidity. As a general formula, it could be said that the domain of the real is greater than or equal to, that is to say contains but is not exhausted by, the domain of the astral. This in turn is greater than or equal to – that is to say, contains but is not exhausted by – the domain of the physical.

L4 is really a preparation for the keynote life L5, to which I turn now.

Life Five: From Galilee to Kashmir – meeting the Master

L5 was born in Galilee about the time of, or shortly after, Jesus' birth, but was soon taken to the Essene headquarters of Qumran. With this his soul was of course already familiar. In this life he was taught by his former pupil, whom he recognises. Among the esoteric teachings freely acknowledged there were doctrines of reincarnation, *karma* and liberation. He is drawn to John the Baptist and is baptised by him, as Jesus was to be. When Jesus begins his mission at about the age of thirty, after himself travelling widely in the Mediterranean and Eastern worlds, L5 feels called to follow him. Close to the disciples, these are times of great inspiration. He studies and practises Jesus' teaching. After the crucifixion he becomes a teacher himself and travels around widely, *inter alia* accompanying Paul to Cyprus.

However, in the years of repression that follow he becomes increasingly full of fear. Then one night twenty years after the crucifixion Jesus appears to him in a dream and summons him to Kashmir, where he is currently teaching. It is unclear to L14 whether the momentous journey east which L5 takes is merely a dream or a reality. (In any event, by now it does not seem to matter.) So our hero begins a momentous journey to meet the Master, in which he undergoes terrible tribulations and in which he is robbed, assaulted and abused, until finally, clad only in a loincloth and armed with his trusty pen, hungry and parched, he arrives at his destination. He meets the Master after a night's sleep. In the following day they walk and talk in the garden by the temple in which he is staying for several hours.

L5 loses his fear and his heart is opened. He is once again full of love, trust and joy in life. Empowered, he returns unafraid, having committed himself with renewed vigour to his mission, Jesus' mission. By opening his heart, Jesus has unblocked the energy locked in his solar plexus and kidneys, which was dammed and unable to express itself in his throat *chakra*. He is now free to speak and act from the heart without fear and full of love, unconditional love and trust in his environment. It is this (Jesus') unconditional love for him which also empowers him to unconditionally love himself and so avoid the perils of attachment and the failure to let go that beset him in L3. In this unconditional love he can find too a perpetual point of peace or tranquillity, the equilibrium which escaped L2 throughout his travels. This L5 now has (despite his equally arduous journeys and schedule). It is this unconditional love which allows him to see and to begin to implement the overcoming of *avidya*, in self-transcendence, in dialectics of inaction and action, as a practical, heart-governed affair. It is this love which gives him the trust to speak and to write, to travel and to teach. (Was this all a dream? If it was a dream it was one with momentous effects. Or was Jesus' resurrection a moment in which his physical body and physical life were actually returned to him so that he could continue his work for a couple more decades in the wake of the Christ-consciousness which had entered him for a few years?)

What is the significance of this journey to meet Jesus aside from its opening of L5's heart *chakra*? We can see the journey itself with its triumphs and tribulations as recapitulating Jesus' fate up to the crucifixion (just as it retraced his subsequent steps) and the love and atonement which Jesus bestows on him as recapitulating the resurrection. Empowered with an open heart and unconditional love and receiving from the Christ-energy the gift of phronesis or practical wisdom or spontaneous right action, he carries out his *dharma*. We see him in secret caves, in underground meetings, in torchlike processions, travelling west and east, north and south as well as in Israel. Indeed he may well have travelled more widely in northern India (another promised land) after his meeting with Jesus in the second great journey from west to east in the book. He dies about the time of the Roman assault on Massada.

The essential teaching of this life is that love unites, heals and expands; fear divides, alienates and contracts. Love is indeed truly the cement of the universe as the philosopher in L6 will proclaim some 1,400 or so years later before embarking on the soul's third journey from west to east to be recorded in this book. But the dialectic of shedding, of disemergence or liberation, is not as yet fully complete. Remnants of a divided mind remain. There is further work to be done. But the Master has shown the way. The soul is now firmly and irrevocably on a path from which it will never stray.

4

THE CEMENT OF THE UNIVERSE AND THE SEARCH FOR YOGA

Life Six: Voyages of discovery – the itinerant cardinal

In L5, our soul had a taste of the Divine (in the form of his meeting with an avatar, or at least a Master, namely Jesus). He is now to be consumed with a passion and desire for a permanent union with the Divine. In a life characterised by the desire to synthesise, transcend and overcome splits and disunity of all kinds, its overriding motif, the dominant passion motivating it, is the desire for union with the principle and source of all union. Animated by a passion to overcome all forms (and sources) of alienation, he seeks to overcome his own alienation from the very principle of de-alienation or union itself. He works his way to an intellectual understanding of God as the cement of the universe, as the source and principle of unconditional love which binds and sustains all things. But he cannot fully realise this principle within himself as his heart, though firing his search, remains unfused with and subordinate to his intellect. And, in a residue of the divided mind of L3, he never succeeds in uniting and synthesising the elements of left and right brain, namely the intellect and intuition respectively. In this life, like L2, he is essentially looking for techniques of self-realisation. Unlike L2, L6 is a synthesiser not an accumulator, but he lacks the direct access to these techniques and their teachers that L2 had at his disposal. He embarks on three voyages of discovery, voyages which are never quite completed (for there remains the work of L7–L9 at the very least to be done), to discover these techniques, glimpsed in Gnostic Christianity but buried by the official church since the time of the Council of Nicaea. These voyages of discovery are (1) from intellect to spirituality; (2) from West to East; and (3) from head to heart. The second voyage is completed in his next incarnation, at least formally in L7, in Japan. The third voyage is completed by the development of unconditional love in L8 and L9. And the first voyage is completed in a spontaneous way in L9 and more methodically in L10 and L11, where he finally succeeds in mastering techniques of self-realisation. In L9–L11 he will succeed in his goal of individual self-realisation, establishing the principle of unity within himself (and at least in L10 and L11 within his own immediate community), but the search for yoga – the principle of all union and de-alienation – inevitably implies a conatus to universal self-realisation and so, on his deathbed in L11, he vows to undertake the return journey from east to west (increasingly the dominant power), entailing through L12–L15 the experience, understanding and projected transcendence of the alienations rife in the socio-economic/political world. The search for union is of course the search for yoga, and the search for it inevitably leads into an enquiry into the principles and techniques of self-realisation. An understanding of their unity involves a grasp, which must be a practical (and not just a theoretical) grasp of their unity. This unity will be a unity in diversity and will involve union itself with the source of all union, the yoga of yogas which is God-realisation.

The life of L6 divides naturally into three phases: first, his childhood, youth and time as a university professor, as an intellectual; second, his period as an active cardinal working mainly within the triangle between Florence, Venice and Genoa, but travelling often to Rome, where he is a close confidante of the Pope, and as far as York (where he mediates a dispute) and the Alhambra in Spain, where he participates in a debate with Spanish, Islamic and Jewish philosophers; and third, the period of his voyage (or voyages) east.

L6 is of course nearly 1,400 years after the end of L5. In the interim many lives have ensued (including some which will be briefly referred to in Italy relevant for L13 and in India relevant for L11), which need not concern us here. Born in northern Italy, near Bologna, to a great and noble family at odds with itself, he quickly becomes adept at mediating and conciliating his way around different parties. This familial background sets the agenda for the dominating concern of his life, overcoming splits and alienations.

Imbued with a passionate and somewhat flamboyant temperament, with a great love of the sciences and arts, and of nature too, and endowed with a spiritual disposition and a mind of tremendous fluency, he sets out to resolve, in his youth and early adulthood, the disputes and divisions raging across the post-Renaissance, so-called 'enlightened' world. An advocate of the newly emerging experimentally informed and rationally inspired post-Aristotelian sciences, he uses his influence and teaches his students to mediate the respective truths of science and religion. He is the negotiator and mediator *par excellence*. Wherever there is a dispute he will set out to settle it, and usually succeed in doing so. But he must settle it on a principled basis. He is opposed to hypocrisy (such as are involved in the sale of indulgences, which he deplores) and half-truths. He is in love with reason, and believes that reason must be one and whole. He is a natural dialectician. He does not really need teachers, being able to see immediately the strength, power, motivation or orientation and weaknesses of any particular position, and how it can be developed towards and synthesised with its opposite in a transcending, more unifying point of view. It is obvious to him that there is a split between the implications of science and the teachings of religion, the immanent beauty of being which reason (and experiment) discloses and the existence of a transcendent God which religion acclaims. But it is equally certain to him that there must be some secret principle of union or synthesis behind this all. He dabbles in Gnostic Christianity and various half-outlawed sects, but is too practically sensible, too much a politician to deviate so circuitously (and to so little obvious effect) with entrenched power and position, which after all holds the great masses of intellectuals and people generally in sway.

He sees the more appropriate road as being to get involved in the affairs of the Church himself. Moreover, his temperament is deeply spiritual and the burning, though unconsummated, desire of his heart is to be at one with God, already identified theoretically as the cement of the universe, the great unifying, binding, healing, expanding power, constituting the force and principle of unity itself. So he takes his vows and quite soon becomes a cardinal. By now he is a close confidante of the Pope, and he travels about Italy at the Pope's request, commissioning works of art and scientific treatises for the benefit of Pope and Church. He has by now developed a powerful system of the unity of being and its unification by God. But he is stuck on what I have called the 'Platonic/Aristotelian fault-line'. There is no way in which a transcendent God can effectively unify the immanent structures of being, but how is God to be made immanent in the world? Through the person of Christ and the power or vocation of the Church, perhaps. But this leaves too big a gap between Christianity and other religions, and between the theory and practice of the Church, not to mention between the Church and the lay people and their institutions. Moreover, it is manifest that the Church is not the unifying force that perhaps the Christ could be. He begins to explore the idea that the same unifying truth is expressed in distorted form in all religions, which he would like to unify under the banner of the energy and teaching which the Christ supremely expressed. He is still, however, looking for a principle of unity which is transcendent to man. And this is the theoretical flaw in his system which reflects the practical failing in his life. The failure to realise that God is immanent in man himself (and especially that he is immanent in L6 himself, and indeed as his Self), immanent and actualised though occluded. The project of realising God is to become what we truly are. And what we truly are is shared – at one with – what each other soul truly is, though we may expect each and every soul to manifest and singularise (individuate) itself in some particular (and more or less unique) set of specific ways.

Through his knowledge of Gnostic Christianity together with his engagements and debates with non-Christian (monotheistic but still essentially transcendent) religious traditions, he has picked up some inkling of the teachings of Vedic and Buddhist philosophy. Perhaps in these esoteric teachings there is a principle of unity that can unite and heal the rupture between his faith (a) in the glory of God and his faith (b) in the powers of reason to explore and depict God's handiwork. Perhaps in them he will find a clue to a subtle level of experience which can unite (a) and (b), or to a level of ontological depth that can harmonise them. At any rate, when the Pope suggests a trip to the East (with trade and conversion equally in mind) he readily consents. The karmic background to this has been laid partly by his previous trips to India in L2 and L5, and partly by a friendship with Marco Polo in a previous Italian life. He has also developed a particular fascination with China and all things Chinese, and his ambition would like to see him set foot on the hitherto effectively closed territory of Japan. So he readily agrees to the Pope's request.

He sets sail from Portugal and works his way down the west coast of Africa, with a large retinue in attendance and an accompanying fleet. He goes ashore on the Gold Coast and has some contact with the locals. He would like to learn more about African philosophies and religions. But the Pope has already summoned him back to settle an important doctrinal dispute with political implications in Vienna. This is just as well, for it is unlikely that his fleet would have made the journey. So in his second attempt he proceeds overland, at least as far as Arabia. He is fascinated by Egypt, and recalls Alexandria and Phebes from a previous life (L2). He continues his trip by sailing across the Indian Ocean from the Arabian peninsula to near Goa, where he disembarks and stays for a period before resuming his trip round the coast of India to the Bay of Bengal, where he disembarks at Calcutta. He would very much like to travel far north to Kashmir and Tibet, but northern India is dangerous territory now with the Mogul invasions at their peak. Moreover, he is not impressed by the pomp and superficial gloss of the Hinduism that he encounters. He is also fired now by an ambition to go even further east, so he sets sail again for China. The means now have begun to overtake the end. His wanderlust has begun to overtake his desire to synthesise. Travelling and exploring for exploration's sake is replacing the search for the principle of unity behind all union, and the principle capable of overcoming disunity between religions and faiths, peoples and men (both within and between men), the principle that would see man as a – the – true *anima mundi* (soul of the world). It is this principle in which he secretly believed but which he could only proclaim if he discovered that God was the soul of man, a discovery which would have to be realised in practice by himself (and to be in principle realisable in practice by all other men). But by now this search for this principle of all union, or rather this practice of all unification, was becoming lost. The means had become the end. Eventually he lands in China and, after some eventful conversations with random Buddhist and Taoist monks and priests and Confucian sages, he dies preaching the Christian gospel on a mound, where his few remaining fellow travellers buried him and on which they placed a simple wooden cross.

He was never to make it to Japan. His mind was almost too quick, too fluent, too synthetic to realise that the principle of all union lay within himself. He was never to *realise* (and so reclaim) his expanded self. What he did do in his writings, great and simple teachings, and in his practical search and quest was to (1) directly persuade many and (2) by exemplification or illustration show other (for example, through a subtle process of amplification (or some other form of contiguous or holistic causality) of like or karmically or heterocosmically or otherwise related) souls of the need for, and set them on the road towards, a principle and a practice, including universally applicable techniques, of self-realisation.

His soul was now fully embarked on the search for yoga, as the immanent cement of the universe which each could find, in his own particular way, within himself. And in so finding help both directly and indirectly the search of all his fellow men, both by at once becoming a better person and more subtly, by having climbed the mountain or trod the path through the forest, making it easier for them to climb or tread (a form of holistic (one–many) amplification).

5

A TAOIST DAWN

Life Seven: The warlord – the Rising Sun and the divided mind

L7 sees the beginning of a several life-long encounter, and indeed love affair, with the figure of the Buddha. But it begins in apparently unpromising circumstances for such an encounter. L6 – of intellectual and physical travel (from mind to spirit and West to East in search of the missing principle of unity) – also determines the location of the next life (L7) in Japan, which sets up the reverse journey from East to West from which the book takes its title. Thus in L7 we see him in Japan as a warlord in a family of warlords, a grand strategist, but with a terrible and fiery temper. The inner anger of L3, fuelled by the frustrations of L6, has exploded into the outer anger of L7. If there is a negative *karma* of abuse it is incurred in this life, but it is also 'fated' in the sense that he is born into a feudal society characterised by conflict, destruction and death, in which only the strongest survive. Moreover, this society is itself at least partially transcended in the course of the life in a gradual spiritual deepening; and the negative *karma* will be more than fully discharged by the lives of loving service in L8 and L9. The divided mind and inner split of L3 is apparent here again, most apparently in the contradiction between the *dharma* or vocation of the soul and its warlike conditions of existence. That this is only an apparent contradiction is however made more than clear by the *Bhagavad Gita*, where it is precisely Arjuna's *dharma* in the particular life concerned to play out his role and fulfil his duties and obligations as a Kshatriya or warrior. The fact that a mind may be split between a sense of its vocation in a spiritual existence and its day-to-day relative conditions of being is a continuing possibility where a soul has karmic burdens to discharge; that is to say, where it must fulfil and/or transcend *karma* imposed by residues or sown by seeds of its past. The divided mind in this life is, however, also divided in the sense of being unfocused and excessively volatile. The excessive querulousness and negative *karma* of abuse is more than repaid by the lives of loving service and the opening of an emergent heart in L8 and L9: that is, the discovery or recovery of the missing principle of union or unity, sought in vain in L6, first in a particularistic form in L8, then in a universalistic form in L9, and finally in the universally accessible forms of L10 and L11. The mind in turn learns to become calm and focused so that activity, if not carefree (as at the dharmic level of spontaneous right action), is at least careful and no longer careless. In particular, the mind learns to become focused in the disciplines of service in L8, the fortitude of patiently born suffering in enlightenment in alienation in L9 and in its thorough immersion in the techniques of mindfulness and meditation in L10 (and later L11). What L7 does contribute to the resolution of the contradiction in L3 is the development of a principle of self-assertiveness, most manifest in the development of the Will. This is a faculty which is not altogether lacking in the intervening lives (especially L6). But it is here developed in an extreme form, the better to be consolidated in the soul's repertoire to deal with life on earth, characterised as it is so strongly by negative emotions, i.e. emotions other than unconditional love and joy. This Will is important for instilling the capacity which I earlier referred to as 'soul force', the capacity of the Self to penetrate and manifest itself in the relative life of man. The other half of the contradiction besetting L3, L3's incapacity to let go, to forgive and unconditionally love (especially herself) is satisfactorily resolved in L8, which is characterised by an attitude of forgiveness, by a giving which does not exclude the agent herself and by a willingness to let bygones be bygones, i.e. to let go of the (persistent) presence of the past.

Fittingly enough, L7 is born in a battleground, as the eldest son to a noble warrior, prosecuting his warlike trade while his mother dies in childbirth. As she dies, she sees on her deathbead the figure of the Buddha shining high in the sky, a figure the innocent soul recognises well from L2. His birth is in a sense his birthright, and encapsulates the contradictions of his life. From an early age he experiences inner frustration, longing for something else, something greater, something nobler, but though he has this longing, he also has the passion and temperament of a warrior and his father readily persuades him into following his predestined (pre-chosen) path. Agile and strong, he quickly becomes adept at the Japanese martial arts. Born to a life of privilege and with a fiery temperament, he cuts his way through childhood, youth and adolescence, making his mark as a warrior-to-be in feudal Japan. But he has a softer side, which manifests itself as a liking for feminine company and a taking of pleasure in the decorative arts. And he feels continually a sort of inner pressure as his life *dharma* to be a warrior is experienced as in conflict with his soul's vocation and his inner peace. He is good at what he does, but he does not like what he is doing. This conflict between his soul's vocation (union with the Divine) and his life *dharma* to be a warrior will occasionally (and increasingly) be experienced as inner frustration, which readily manifests itself in outward anger and other expressions of his fiery temperament and unsettled, unfocused, divided mind. This last characteristic has the consequence that while if a conflict is short he will normally win it, if it is protracted he is almost certain to lose. He thus both overreacts and reacts too quickly and as a strategist can formulate, but not execute, his plans. Painfully aware of this contradiction and weakness he seeks out advice and help. He has a general (KP) who has been a practitioner of Zen and indeed spent several years in a Zen monastery. Gradually, under the patient counsel of this general, he comes to see that there are gentler, simpler and calmer ways of being and doing (accomplishing things), including success at warfare. To a degree he becomes more focused, and quietens down when he marries a much younger woman (aged 16) – the Alexandrian love of his life (T) in L2 – but he remains inwardly restless. It is as if his soul's drive in the single-minded pursuit of God, which requires a life of balanced and integrated activity, was somehow to be replaced by the single-minded pursuit of every transient whim or sleight, real or imagined. His pride – pride is a symptom of an ego which refuses to see itself as dialectically developing into something other than itself (albeit also in essence nothing other than it already always was) – his pride is easily stung. There is too little *yin* in his *yang*, too little give in his take.

One day all this changes. He is caught in an ambush in the mountains in the snows, badly wounded and left for dead. He crawls to a nearby monastery, where he is tended by the monks. He reconciles himself to his condition (an acceptance hitherto lacking in his life) and begins patiently to read their texts. One day he sees the Buddha reflected in a pond as the ice begins to melt; the next day, floating high above the mountain tops. The next night he is sitting in his room poring over some ancient texts when, falling asleep, his head thuds against the book he is reading, his third eye opens and he has a vision of the very different (L4) Essene life of simplicity, purity, joy and service. Here, for a moment, in L14's time machine, two lives merge: the symbol of both lives is the sun, here in L7 the rising sun, which sets up a poignant echo of that Essene life with its very different timbre. The next day his faithful general (KP) visits him in the monastery and is amazed to see the transformation he has apparently and so suddenly undergone. L7 now becomes the most ardent possible practitioner and student of Zen and takes his vows in the monastery, sacrificing the privileges of his feudal past. He is seemingly a transformed character. However, lust and love for his young wife take him back. He spends a few brief days in his home; and decides once more to leave. On his way out he changes his mind again. Caught between the absolute and relative, he is frozen. He loses his nerve and decides to stay as a warlord, but adopts a more retiring and circumspect role. He never lets go, however, of the vision he has had of the Buddha or of that other life in some far-off country; and he spends the next couple of months planning an extended trip west to China and thence to Tibet and to India (trips that will in fact be undertaken eventually in L8, L9, L10 and L11). But these trips never materialise. Soon after their formulation he dies in combat, pierced by an arrow through his heart. His death, like his birth, is apocryphal, caught in a contradiction between the demands of the absolute (his *dharma*) and the relative (his inherited *karma*). He has however, in the course of fulfilling this *karma*, developed the will to make a decisive choice and an opening in the East where he can learn the techniques of uniting absolute and relative, transcending this apparent contradiction by embedding the absolute in the relative, the unmanifest in the day-to-day flux of relative being. This is the middle truth which L7 will practise in L8 and teach in L9.

What is the teaching, the lesson, of this life? One can merely receive or gratefully accept and learn from, or better still transcend, one's *karma*. Fulfilling or discharging the karmic obligation is an opportunity to learn from it and to sow the seeds for its future transcendence. This is the path that L7 takes. He sets in motion the trajectory of L8 to L11. He was not able, however, in L7, given his fieriness and lack of focus, to settle immediately into a life of practising the techniques of concentration and contemplation, meditation and mindfulness, which he would learn again in L9, L10 and L11. First his fieriness (fire, *agni*, his outward anger, that is, his anger against himself turned outwards on to the world), had to be assuaged and dissipated by a life of total unconditional love for himself and for all other beings. The only response to anger, which is just self-hatred turned against the world, is complete unconditional love and forgiveness. This is the lesson that will be practised in L8 and L9, as the negative *karma* of L7 is at once discharged and transcended by that spontaneous right action, which is acquired by being practised, which comes ultimately from being embedded in every moment of one's being in one's transcendental Self.[1] L7, then, has seen the Will released, but its exercise as yet uncontrolled. The soul is, however, now ready more tenaciously to imprint itself in its incarnations, to embed itself more fully in the relative domain of being.

Life Eight: In China I – the emergent heart and a life in bondage

L6–L9 are about the search for union with the divine. L6–L11 are about overcoming alienation, ultimately in the formulation, in L10 and more especially in L11, of the project of universal self-realisation. As already remarked, the *karma* of L7 is paid (and transcended) in L8 and L9. The inner conflict of L3 is resolved in

1 Such action is maximally coherent, maximally creative and maximally compassionate; thus maximally evolutionary or progressive for both the individual soul and for others.

the unconditional love and service and forgiving, the letting go of the past in L8;[2] while L6's search for the principle of union, essentially enlightenment, is satisfied, if only fleetingly and transiently in the life of L9, to be consolidated in L10 and especially L11.

L8, like L3, is partially about the fate of women; and like L3, it shows the suppression and suffering, but also the strength, of womenkind. It isolates very clearly the abuse of male power as structural sin. More generally, however, it is about the abuse of power and forgiveness. It is also about the *Tao*, the way as manifest in service and industry, balanced in multiple activity, including flexibility as well as concentration, that is, multiple (plural) mindfulness in concentrated activity. And finally, it is about such service, forgiveness and strength in a heart which does nothing but or except in the name of the Buddha or of Quan-Yin, the Madonna-like Buddhist Bodhisattva of mercy or compassion.

L8 is born as a woman to a peasant family in southern China. She is regarded by her family, and especially her father, who regularly beats and abuses her, as a liability and is sold into a richer household when she reaches puberty. She grows up without education and is used and abused by this new household for profit. She works in a sweatshop making writing instruments (and related goods, inks and paint brushes and the like), cooks and cleans, tends the pigs, and feeds and looks after wild boar and the domestic animals of the household. After some time her erstwhile suitor and abuser readily begins to rent her out to other men, attracted by her beauty and industry, for their pleasure. Finding only intermittent refuge in a love affair which had begun in this way, she eventually dies of exhaustion in her mid-forties. Let me expand a bit on this brief account of her life.

She has no education formally, but she is teaching herself how to read and write. She wears an amulet of the Buddha, and everything she does is dedicated to the Buddha. This amulet is given to her by the love of her life, her male companion from L4 (AC), who worked with her then on the Dead Sea Scrolls. Together, they study Buddhist texts. There is mutual recognition between them, just as they both recognise the Buddha as their master. Though she does not actually 'see' Essene days, she has an intimation of them, and of her previous work and friendship with her companion. She does nothing except in the name of the Buddha or of Quan-Yin. She would like to learn and study more but, hardworking as well as beautiful, she is too busy, both sustaining the household and being exploited (in effect being used by its head as a prostitute for profit). She bears no grudges (every grudge is an imprisonment by the past). She is always trying to learn from life; given a situation, she will ask, 'what can it teach me?' Thus she breaks a vase, scattering it into fragments, in her first home and the father who

2 In the transcendence of bitterness symbolically manifest L3's predeliction for sour fruits: oranges and lemons.

will sell her beats her for it. Later, that same father visits her in her new household in disguise. Indeed she sees her love for herself as the fount of her love for others. She sees through it and forgives him. She does not fail to love herself either. She has learned the secret of natural contraception and will feign illness in order to avoid the risk of conception. However, she does have a daughter by a lusty scholarly gentleman (B), who finds her a pleasant distraction from his studies and engages in a duel for her affections with a rival (KP), a military man with great stamina in bed. The duel is a bit of a farce; the military man does not turn up, while the scholar has hired a servant to shoot him from behind a bush in case he were to do so.

The principle that above all guides her is that everything has, contains, to some degree, a Buddha nature; and every person, situation or thing reveals to a greater or lesser degree its Buddha aspects (though abused, she knows herself, because she has the Buddha nature to be a Bodhisattva-in-the-making). She does, thinks and says nothing except in the name of the Buddha and she wears her amulet of the Buddha constantly. This Buddha-being is a real (causally aefficacious present) absence within the flux of manifest experience. It is a void, vanishing point, moment of peace. As the absolute stands to the relative, so in the principles guiding her life does emptiness, the point represented by the Buddha or the Bodhisattva Quan-Yin, stand to the manifest. She will begin to discover in her extreme business, industriousness, the most peace (still, quiet, calm). This absence or emptiness is itself a dynamic force which, like a dance, or as in Tai Chi or the Chinese adjective (which is never a property but always a process) – this emptiness – is always the centre of a hive of activity, of creation *ex nihilo*. She is devoted to Quan-Yin and prays every night to her for time to study and the opportunity perhaps to make a trip to Tibet and India. Each night she burns incense to Quan-Yin. She reflects how she would have liked to have studied more and to have expounded the principles she has discovered in her practical life, to have spent more time on soul work and to have been born free. She bears, however, no resentment and her wishes will be fulfilled in L9–L11.

In her life she comes to learn, and to know when to act and when not to act, i.e. to inact; that inaction, such as silence, can be effective; and how to act by inacting rather than acting.[3]

3 This is inaction in the sense of spontaneous or basic-like right action. That is inaction in the sense of acting spontaneously so that all action becomes 'basic', without effort or mediation (or even thought, so to speak), rather than inaction in the sense of meditation or ontological retreat. Accordingly she learns how to act with least effort, dispersal of energy (how to do less and accomplish more, how the little can produce the big); how it is the *yin* in the *yang* (or vice versa) that balances it; she learns how it is the absence, void or emptiness that creates coherence (the hole in the pot or vase that keeps it whole); how to mobilise *chi* (for example, in self-healing or in relation to male sexual energy) at a glance, by the power of silence or

She also learns that love is the supreme principle of life. That mindfulness in the moment is consistent with (1) a multiplicity of activities and (2) integration of her being. She learns that acceptance does not imply resignation, but rather that to transform the world entails understanding and accepting it just as it is. Moreover, she learns that she can learn about the world just by observing it (and herself, the point of observation); and not only that changing the world depends upon observing it but also that she can change it just by observing it. It is obvious enough that a conversation can have material effects. Thought, or *chi* (energy), manifest in the form of consciousness, informs the conversation, just as it forms the machine, which produces real material effects on another thing or being, or more generally, the world. Moreover, one cannot change the world tautologically, except by acting (or inacting) oneself. This itself presupposes or includes an act performed by (if not necessarily immediately upon) oneself. So tautologically and obviously, the first step in changing the world is to change oneself; and conversely, by changing oneself one begins to change the world. This can happen in a linear or holistic way, and in a gross or subtle manner. Finally, L8 discovers that the only response to suffering is joy in union with the Divine, which itself entails activity to absent that suffering and its causes, causes which ultimately lie themselves in alienation from the Divine. In this way, joy in union with the Divine will also lead to joy in union with all manifestations of the Divine – the plenitude of being.

If L6 and L7 are lives of power, L8 and L9 are lives of apparent powerlessness. But L8 has discovered the secret of apparent powerlessness, that it is upon the creativity of slaves in abusive power or master–slave relationships that all wealth and production, including the reproduction of that very relationship, and therefore the open possibility of its transformation, ultimately depends. L8 has come to terms with life and has acquired mastery of the arts of love and forgiveness (including self-love and self-forgiveness), making them her own, but she cannot systematise or universalise her practical skills in the way she would like to do, although no doubt they have subtle heterocosmic and karmic effects on others. She has reached, in the point of still or emptiness within the business of her life, an equilibrium point which corresponds to what I have been calling 'ontological access' in the structure of dialectics of inaction among techniques of self-realisation.

thought; the art of balance, and the unity of opposites, their necessary co-existence and their transformative implosions into each other; the secret of Indra's net, in the bedroom, in the kitchen, in the workshop, in life generally, namely that what is involved is a holistic performance or co-production; the practice of giving (and not just taking) including giving to herself and forgiving herself and others; the essentially practical nature of the way of self-realisation or overcoming *avidya* or ignorance. But though this is something essentially to be done, we need not conclude from that that it is as such ineffable. Indeed, L9 will speak the truth (though eventually become disenchanted with speaking, rather than merely just being, it) which L8 and L9 both practise.

But she would like to enunciate and formulate this; for the way, the *Tao* is not ineffable, though its essence may be silence (to confound the two is to commit a variant of the epistemic fallacy). Moreover, she cannot claim to have the time or freedom in her life to fully implement and embed this equilibrium point in the totality of her being; rather it is something she never loses sight of and seeks to achieve ever more so. She would like to systematise and universalise her practical skills, to deepen her self-realisation, to avoid those discrepancies of theory and practice and the alienations that come from her being the slave of others. She would like this for all, and she would like to be able to show this for all, in particular to speak (and write) with the freedom with which she was empowered by Jesus in L5. All these wishes will be granted in L9. But L9 shares with L8 three weaknesses. First, the degree and manner of self-realisation is too immediate (the middle truth is too under-differentiated and unmediated), too unsystematic and haphazard to be universally communicated as accessible and it is in both cases achieved in social alienation. The rectification of these weaknesses will be the arduous work of L10 to L15. L10 will systematise techniques of self-realisation, L11 will formulate conditions and a project for their universal accessibility; and L12–L15 will seek to realise this project and in so doing achieve the goal of L6 of overcoming all alienation, in particular in the project of universal self-realisation in unity-existence.

Life Nine: In China II – the middle truth – in search of balance, the dynamic being of emptiness and enlightenment in alienation

I start with a brief description of L9. In it the soul is reborn as a male, again in China but further west in Szechwan province. Naive, vulnerable and somewhat effeminate (infused with *yin* energy), he leaves home and his mandarin parents at an early age, having being well schooled in all the systems of Chinese philosophy, to write poetry and fathom the mysteries of the universe. But he finds himself scorned for his radical and naturalist Taoist philosophy (into which he wishes to inject an element of spirituality and openness). Abused and neglected, he travels throughout the Chinese world, finding solace only in nature, dreams of a beautiful woman and occasional conversations with sympathetic Buddhist and Taoist monks. Though a well-known Taoist priest, this life, like L5 and L8, is about rejection, the abuse of power, but also, like L5, it is about the opening of the heart *chakra*. This is the first life of enlightenment. But though the Chinese poet has the truth, there is no one to hear it. He dies young, lost in contemplation of the beauty of a rose, symbol of enlightenment and love, reflected in water. It is this rose that is captured in the cover of the book.

The principle of L9's life and teaching as a life of enlightenment in alienation is that the absolute or in Taoist terminology emptiness or the void or the unmanifest or (to use the more Vedic term) the absolute is manifest everywhere, just by being and in the here and now, in the incessant flux and flow of everyday life. Its weaknesses have already been indicated:

1 it is too immediate, that is emptiness and its manifestation in the flux are both differentiated and mediated in countless different ways;
2 it is too haphazard and unsystematic, in particular it is not related to a practice of inaction or meditation which could stabilise it and facilitate its communication or spread to others;[4] and
3 it is itself propagated in a situation of alienation, that is without an audience, i.e. there is no one to hear the message,[5] since he is alienated from his community.

These three weaknesses are not unconnected. He is alienated partly because he refuses to take, in practice as well as in theory, social mediations (such as that given by the Confucian concept of the state mandate of heaven) seriously. This is a real weakness in his system and the dialectic that *From East to West* describes will have to remedy this in L12–L15 through the experience and understanding of the socio-economic/political world if the project of universal self-realisation, formulated in L11, that is, of the Self as totality, is to be completed. Without social mediations, the dialectic is radically complete. Among these social mediations are an appreciation of the need for universally accessible and stabilised, communicable techniques of self-realisation, and L9's refusal to enunciate any such techniques is in violation, as already noted, of standard Buddhist and Buddhist-influenced Chinese practice. The middle truth may be the truth, but it must be in accordance with reason and communicable, and related to the pre-existing practices and traditions of those L9 will seek to engage in it.

Still he speaks. He faces down and overcomes his fear. His heart is open and his throat *chakra* active: he expresses himself clearly, although he does not communicate his message accessibly. He has however learned the lesson of L5, which both recapitulated the fate and retraced the steps of Jesus. Though a Taoist in this life, he is empowered by the Buddha, and he sees no conflict between Buddhist and Taoist principles. Indeed, he often sees the Buddha everywhere, literally, not like L8, just metaphorically. Above all, he sees him meditating high above the

4 Thus it violates an important principle of in particular Chinese Buddhist tradition, which is always to tie a principle, teaching or practice to a particular type of meditation or meditative practice.

5 Everyone is concerned (or so it seems to him) with ceremony, ritual and stereotyped performance (*li* as performance) whether the role being played is that of the gentleman, the superior man or the sage.

mountains, in reality or in his creative imagination in the Himalayas. This is a vision which he can conjure up at will, but it never ceases to inspire him. The Buddha is pulsing through his heart.

In traditional Chinese terms, we could say that L8 has *li* (etiquette) and *ren* (human heartedness) but suffers from a lack of reciprocity (*shu*) and is not wise in the sense of a scholar (*ru*). L9, on the other hand, is eagerly prosecuting the virtues of wisdom and scholarliness in daring to think on the basis of *ren* a thorough unmasking of *li* (etiquette) and the scholarly, sagely, superior role playing that his Confucian adversaries engage in. He is a non-conformist, a radical, a poet with a mystic identification with the cosmos who can see truth and beauty, the great ultimate, everywhere without the mediation of the supposed 'mandate of heaven' given to the state and the powers-that-be. He is not alienated from God or nature, but he is alienated from the community and society in which he lives. In contrast in L10 he is not socially alienated, in the sense that he is a dedicated member of a community of Buddhist monks, but in that life he is alienated from part of his soul nature. He is restricted, not given sufficient individuality, freedom, singularity, to roam intellectually and spiritually. In this life (L9) he roams around the Chinese world writing poems, making money performing priestly functions and teaching the idea of God-in-nature without the state mandate of heaven. He is Taoist but naturalist and spiritual, almost radically egalitarian. He is utterly opposed to Confucianism of any sort. He wants to synthesise Taoism and Buddhism, and identifies the Buddhist void or *nirvana* and the Taoist ultimate or dynamic being of emptiness. With a weakish disposition and somewhat effeminate in appearance, he is abused and scorned. He has excelled in his youth in the entire repertoire of Chinese philosophy, but now he is no longer interested in scholarly niceties or intellectual pieties but the simple truth of being. He does not, however, disdain to debate with neo-Confucians. He is tireless in argument, but his argument always ends with the same point: the immediacy and omnipresence (ubiquity) of the dynamic being of the great void. He spends much time debating and talking with Buddhist and Taoist monks. He may be seeking to embed the absolute in the relative, but he is not embedded in his society. He is cheated and robbed, beaten and raped, flogged and imprisoned for a spell. He has dreams, visions of romance, of a beautiful woman (also like his coming enlightenment, reflected in the rose), but despite several love affairs cannot find it. He travels isolated throughout the Chinese world. He comes to feel that only non-attachment, including non-attachment to his own avowed standpoint, can end suffering. He wants to travel to Tibet and India. He begins his final trip and dies enlightened, engulfed by the thought, or rather the being designated by the thought, that it is enough to just be and so non-be without needing to preach or proclaim the presence of the dynamic presence of absence or being of non-being.

He dies looking at the reflection of a rose in water on his way to Tibet, where he is to be born in L10. This rose symbolises for him everything he would like to say, and yet says it more eloquently. So in the end his enlightenment is sudden and solipsistic. In some sort of poetic justice, he has realised the truth but cannot speak it, for the truth just is the way, and the way is being. It will take several more lifetimes before he can teach as well as display this. For as we have seen, there is no incompatibility in a truth and its statement. The statement may be spoken in the spirit of and in the truth which it expresses. This is not to confound or identify the two. Rather, on the contrary, the intelligibility of this depends upon there being a level separation between the statement and the truth it at once both expresses and exemplifies (or instantiates).

Enlightenment for L9 is to see the being of non-being (the void, emptiness, absence) and beyond or within it, the creative void or the great ultimate, the dynamic being of the most pure non-being which is the source of all the forces and energies, the seasons and elements and the world of ten thousand things just in that world of the ten thousand things, of change, of flux; to see emptiness in the whole of manifest creation and to see it immediately as well as everywhere. This is tantamount to seeing the Buddha nature everywhere and to seeing the Buddha nature in the dynamic flux as one thing never ceases to change into another, opposites interpenetrating all the while in a world of flowing process in which stillness or repose can only be found as poetry in motion. In this world, moreover, everything is, to adopt our terms not only second edge, 2E, but also third level, 3L. The world is formed like Indra's net, a glittering necklace of jewels, in which each reflects into each other and the whole reflects back into each and itself. Holistic causality incorporates a generalised principle of heterocosmic affinity between the members of Pythagorean dyads or bi-polar opposites such as part–whole, inner–outer, microcosm–macrocosm, upper–lower, individual and collectivity; male and female, *yin* and *yang*; absolute and relative. Such heterocosmic causality, which may operate in a subtle and non-manifest way, from the obvious amplification of microscopic or individual changes on to a population or collectivity or the macrocosm (and vice versa) to more recondite aefficacies. Moreover, from a generalised holistic perspective we both change the universe by changing a single cell and cannot change a single cell without changing the universe. Closely connected to this theme is the principle of balance necessitating the presence of the polar opposite in the sphere of a being or aspect to sustain it; and if, as in Chinese thought, the whole is set in motion, then we have the continual flowing of *yin* into *yang*, the continual expansion and contraction or explosion and implosion of the universe. The continual collapse and regeneration of life and consciousness from the void, of *li* or form from *chi* or energy. In L9's thought, for all his personal singlemindedness (and perhaps because of it), we are moving very close to the terrain of dialectical critical realism.[6]

6 The principle of karmic impartiality and equilibriation applied to heterocosmic relata (such as Pythagorean dyads, couples, oppositions, polyads, agents and so on) leads to the prevalence of the phenomena of role reversal. Thus the powerlessness of L8 and L9 is succeeded by the spiritual power of L11 and the secular or material power of L12. There are constant swings and oscillations, so that no Self can get stuck in a particular ego. Thus the humiliations and poverty of L8 give way to the pomp and riches of L12, the isolation experienced in L9 to the fame and entourage enjoyed in L11, the fluency of L11 to the hesitancy of L13, the doubts and splits of L14 to the confident syntheses of L15, the fear of L5 to the trust of L9 or L15. Furthermore, as Taoist thought maintains the presence of an opposite is a necessary constituent of any element, you can easily see how for each balance or virtue, there are two vices: the presence of this opposite in excess or in deficiency. This is the true rationale of the doctrine of the mean.

6

AT THE HEARTBEAT OF THE BUDDHA

Life Ten: In Tibet – a Himalayan heartbeat – or compassion and the void

The theme of this life is the move from, compatibility of and indeed tendential mutual implication of individual liberation and universal self-realisation. In L11, this move will imply a move from the path of renunciation to the path of action, and in L12 and subsequent lives from the way of the recluse to the way of the householder. L10 is, however, firmly a recluse and firmly on the path of renunciation. More generally, L6–L9 have been about the search for union with the Divine, whereas L10–L15 are about the integration of the Divine in life and the search for the union of the Divine-in-the-community. L10 is also about the culmination of a yogic engagement, which began in L7 (and indeed before it in L2), with the Buddha. All lives L8–L12, however, have at the centre a cosmic beloved, an object of complete and utter devotion. And all involve, though in different ways, two kinds of ontological access: meditation or ascent of consciousness to the absolute; and prayer, worship, communion or grace, namely the experience of the manifestation of the absolute in some relative form, the descent of spirit if you like. These two aspects of yogic experience are of course symbiotically related, though different traditions will emphasise one or the other. Moreover, in L10 the contradiction between the *dharma* of the soul and the *karma* imposed by its life circumstances tends to be attenuated. The soul force, so weak in L3, is realised in an undivided mind manifest in focused activity. This activity, though focused, will be unattached, because the source of all inner conflict, whether expressed in some outward form such as anger or not, is attachment. The rampant and wild will of L7 has, to use terms drawn from the Buddha's noble eightfold path, become focused by right effort in L8 and L9, to be reinforced by right mindfulness and right meditation in L10 (and subsequently L11). There is still, however, here a contradiction between absolute and relative reality; or rather the absolute, which is unbounded, finds itself manifest in a restricted and partial way. The soul has the acceptance and recognition which was denied him in L9, that is, he is no longer alienated from his community, but his community is still alienated from much of the rest of the world.

This sets the scene for the debate which was raging through the Sangha, the monastic order which the Buddha founded and of which L10 was a member, between the proponents of (individual) *liberation* and those of *compassion*. In the end L10 took the momentous vow, along with many others, to postpone his release from the round of rebirth, i.e. *nirvana*, until the realisation of all beings was achieved in what I have called 'unity existence'. This is the path of the Bodhisattva and it will lead to a re-engagement with the material, physical, socio-economic world in L12 to L15, where there are karmic residues and unfinished business still to be cleared up, before both an individual self-realisation and complete and total orientation to the project of universal self-realisation can be attained. From this standpoint, which was already prefigured by the understanding of L10, individual self-realisation and the project of universal self-realisation mutually implied each other. For on the one hand individual liberation was impossible without the virtue of compassion, and in particular an orientation to help the liberation of others and more generally the relief of suffering everywhere – that ubiquitous phenomenon (suffering) whose cause and cure the Buddha had so pellucidly pinpointed. On the other hand the liberated human being would naturally, acting from the standpoint of *dharma* or spontaneous right action, act in the most compassionate way, namely to relieve (or minimise) suffering and help both (a) immediately (holistically) in virtue of his very liberation (in a subtle, heterocosmic, reflexive way) and (b) mediately through the performance of spontaneous right acts to secure the liberation of all other beings.

But there was another problem. The very pellucidness of the way in which the Buddha had foregrounded attention on the fact of suffering and his realisation that its cause, ultimately ignorance or *avidya* underpinning desire, craving or thirst, and its cure were both *practical* matters – and matters of momentous urgency – had led him to refuse to engage in metaphysical speculations about the nature of karmic connections or explicitly to posit an underlying continuant, namely the soul, which was the subject of repeated incarnations. This is a serious problem for Buddhist epistemology. However, on a dispositional realist account the soul as an underlying, relatively ultimate, continuant can be analysed just as a disposition or power (which may be as concretely singularised or individuated, that is as complex and elaborated as you like). More particularly it is a conjugate of dual dispositions: to be embodied in successive layers of embodiment, and in particular at the physical level, over a succession of lives; and to be disembodied or free i.e., to return, in self-consciousness, and after the experience of the oppositionalities, limitations and emotions of the relative (including demi-real) realm of being to its basic self as spirit. The soul's journey through its incarnations is a voyage freely undertaken, but it is a voyage with only one possible eventual outcome: realisation or enlightenment, as spirit or God-stuff is the most basic or deepest (most extensive, most enduring) categorial structure of the finite, bounded created world, including all its limitations, frustrations and experiences. It is worth stressing that to say that a soul is a disposition or a complex of dispositions is not to say that it does not exist in its own right. Rather, dispositional realism accentuates the ontological priority of the possible and refuses to delimit the domain of the real to that which is actualised, in terms of some or other (current) criterion of actuality.

This resolution of the question of the reality of the bearer of karmic connections between incarnations does not of course solve the question of the forms of being of the soul between incarnations, which is outside the scope of the present book. Within its scope, however, lies a problem unresolved by the resolution of the debate between the advocates of individual liberation and those of universal compassion. For liberation had to be possible for those outside the Sangha; the *dharma* had to be communicable to those on the path of action, following the way of the householder, the busy bees at work in the relative world of existence. And if it was to incorporate dialectics of inaction, it had to do so in a way other than by promising them, as a result of a life of virtue, their own spell in some monastic order. The way or the teaching had to be applicable outside the monastery or the ashram.[1]

The restrictiveness, if not of the teaching then certainly of the practice, of Mahayana and Vajrayana Buddhism was both experienced as such by L10 and reflected a feeling of restrictedness in his own life. He wanted to travel spiritually, intellectually, physically, if only better to spread the *dharma*. He wanted to explore and break boundaries and borders in search of a grasp of the concrete universality = singularity of man.

It will be remembered that there were three basic problems with L9's 'middle truth'. First, it was too unsystematic and haphazard to be universally accessible. Second, it was under-differentiated both in its conception of the absolute or the unbounded or emptiness and in its conception of the relative or phenomena or flux. And third, it was formulated in alienation from the community it was supposed to inform. It is worth stressing that both the absolute and relative realms are differentiated. There is no reason to suppose that the absolute is not subject to all manner of absolute differentiations, mediations, differences and levels of depth, degrees of extension and so on. And it is patently obvious that the

1 This remains so even if, in a world of growing self-realisation, levels of abundance and self-sufficiency which minimised the need for relative activity, and even more conflict, were attainable.

relative world is open, structured, differentiated, changing, mediated; subject to different degrees of penetration or forms of manifestation by the absolute and conversely overlain by differential degrees of error, evil and structural sin. To say this is not to say that totalities and in particular the totality that constitutes the self-sufficiency, autonomy or freedom of enlightenment need necessarily be complex or elaborate: totalities may be simple and pure. En-lightenment may be *light* (the result of much shed). Totalities must however be complete. Any relevant absence or omission will generate an alienation or split. Such a split will need to be transcended in a greater re-totalisation. This is the driving impulse behind the desire, which becomes increasingly insistent through L10 and L11, to universalise in a concrete (concretely universal) and dialectically accessible way. That point of retreat or rather vantage point, free from all contradictions and splits, which would amount to union with the principle and source of all union in L6's terms, which our soul had sought, glimpsed and even experienced fleetingly in previous lives, now had to be at once firmly embedded in his own relative being and at the same time universally accessible to all other beings. This is the project which will animate the rest of the lives described in the book.

In L10, the soul has moved across the borders to Tibet. Let me briefly describe his life there. He enters a Buddhist monastery at a young age and becomes adept at the techniques of meditation and mindfulness. In contrast to L9, he here experiences acceptance, gaining recognition, and begins to instigate reforms in the theory and practice of Mahayana Buddhism. He plays a leading part in the debates that are raging through the Sangha. Of a highly devotional nature, the figure of the Buddha, meditating high over the Himalayas but beating close to his heart, is a constant presence in his life, as it has been in previous ones and will recur again. Though his third eye and crown *chakra* are open, he again experiences frustration, this time at the rigidities of the theory and practice of the various monastic orders, even though he plays a large and influential role within them. He longs for the freedom of spirit and expression of the Indian sages he has met, who can apparently think and do anything. So it is no surprise when in his next life he is reincarnated in India. Although frustrated, he is not bitter, he is too devoted to the *dharma* for this. We see him (through L14's time machine) sitting, sipping butter tea, chatting with his fellow monks about all manner of topics, travelling about the Buddhist world (including a return eastwards to China and Japan, where he revels in the mastery of debates and the resolution of *koans*), joking with children in the streets, even playing rudimentary football. He rises to a position of some authority and begins to prepare for a pilgrimage to the holy sites of the Buddha's life in India. But he dies in peaceful meditation before he is able to embark on this journey.

7

TRANSCENDENCE AND TOTALITY: OR SALTED LASEE WITH THE GURU

Life Eleven: In India – the Guru – or from the path of renunciation to the path of action

As we have seen, L10 longed for the freedom of spirit and expression of the Indian sages and gurus he had met (a freedom similar to that which he had experienced in China in L9 but in India with apparently greater tolerance for diversity of thought), who could apparently think, say and do anything. Moreover, at the time of his death he was preparing for a trip to India. So it was natural that in L11 he should reincarnate in India. He had indeed already had many Indian lives, including one as a devout peasant, another as a temple dancer, a third as a neophyte in an ashram and a fourth as a practitioner in a tantric order, all coming chronologically between L5 and L6 in this book. The last two of these lives had been lived out under the sign of Shiva, and Shiva is to be a major presence in this life too. But, although he will be eclectic and catholic to the core, in this life he is born to a Vaisnavite family, and the presiding deity that runs throughout it is the figure of Krishna. However, even as a youth he has both Muslim and Christian spiritual experiences. He is from an early age in adoration of the Mother Divine (in one of the outbuildings of the temple dedicated to whom he, in his late adolescence, regularly engages in tantric practices) and he later works for a time in a traditional Saivite monastery, studying Vedic texts and writing commentaries on them. However, in this life he is destined to become a guru with his own ashram. The ashram will become huge (containing many notable figures in their own right and many others with whom he has more or less deep karmic connections) and wherever he goes he is surrounded by a large, if ramshackle, entourage. A massive consciousness, he instigates various reforms within the Hindu corpus on the basis of his own original studies of Vedic philosophy. He wishes for religious and political transformation, and criss-crosses the country debating inside and outside his ashram with other gurus (such as M) on the need for truth and change. As a spiritual teacher of considerable renown, he has a massive following, holding a huge swathe of Hindu India in the palm of his hand, but he realises that there is little he can do against the growing power of the West without a spiritual, cultural and intellectual revolution. And so he forms the intention on his deathbed to teach Vedic truth to the West (and in so doing, renounces the scorn in which he has held it since his Japanese and Chinese lives). This desire sets up the remaining rounds of lives in the book and can only be completed when he becomes a successful and recognised philosopher in the West, so that he can then, like Moses, take both East and West to the promised land, crossing the Rubicon to a world of abundance without scarcity, or fulfilment without suffering, the immanentisation of heaven on earth.

I have already noted that in his youth he had Muslim and Christian experiences as well as a multiplicity of kinds of Hindu ones. He is convinced of the essential unity of mankind, and indeed of all religions and faiths. (So much so that he does not hold back from identifying the Christ as a purer or higher form of manifestation or energy of God than the denizens of the Hindu corpus.) His belief in the essential unity of mankind, which he grounds in their common categorial essence as God-stuff or spirit (through which he sees, unlike Shankara, as concretely singularised or individuated in myriad ways).[1] Believing in the essential unity of man he was appalled by the splits which beset humanity, splits within and between peoples and faiths. Thus there was the unjustifiable and antiquated caste system, a growing class structure and the continuing oppression of women. On all these issues he took a radical stance. He implied moreover that individual self-realisation entailed an immediate practical commitement or conatus to their overthrow. This we can understand as a natural corollary of the dialectic of desire, which is also from attachment generally, to freedom. This dialectic takes two forms – individual and universal – and though the former is its necessary condition, without the latter the former remains incomplete. Caste, class and gender were the proximate source of just some of the social splits – others were generational, familial, regional, occupational and so on – within Hindu India. But there was also the splits between Hinduism, Islam and Christianity and the communal conflicts that the split between Hindu and Muslim India generated. Then there were the splits between Hinduism and all the other faiths of the world, and the increasingly prominent split within India between the growing power of the West, and British rule in particular, and native Indian aspirations and opportunities. The West itself for its part was a source of splits and alienations between competing powers, firms (within capitalism), classes, parties, regions and interests of all

1 There is an apocryphal story concerning Shankara. One day Shankara was challenged by a beggar or outcast as to why he avoided him. How could Shankara justify this when they all shared the same Self, *Atman* or soul?

sorts. Moreover, there was the split between science and religion, a split that L11 regarded as ill-founded and corrigible once the immaturity of the former and the ossification of the latter had been overcome. In particular, a transcendental account of science and an immanent account of (the basis of) religion could be shown to reconcile them.

At the core of L11's work and teaching was the idea of the essential unity-in-diversity of God (complemented by the notion of the concrete singularity of man). This unity underlay different forms of manifestation, a multiplicity of different experiences of God. So we have ontological realism and experiential (or epistemological) relativism about God. But God was not, or not just, transcendent. He was also immanent in being, and in particular immanent as the essential categorial structure or intrinsic nature of each and every man. This grounded the idea of the essential unity of mankind, and hence of different faiths. Moreover, the notion of God as both transcendent and immanent (and when transcendent, as manifestable in the relative field in a multiplicity of different ways) resolved the aporia within Hinduism between belief in an absolute without qualities accessible in yogic meditation and belief in a personal Lord such as Krishna or Shiva or some other deity – essentially the dispute between Shankara and Ramanuja – and reconciled the two forms of ontological access that I earlier differentiated, namely meditation and prayer or grace. In this way, the two branches of Vedic Hinduism were united and Buddhism was brought closer to Christianity and, in a different (more mediated) way, Islam. There is both the God within and the God without, both an absolute accessible in meditation and realisable, in enlightenment, in the relative field (by dialectics, and associated techniques, of self-realisation) – this is the God within – and our personal Lord (or Lady) accessible in prayer and by His or Her grace, a manifestation of the transcendent in the relative field. The task of life was to realise this God within which, when realised, and when the subject had discharged all his *karma*, would make him one with God himself, or, put another way, a God in his own right – God-realisation (the former emphasis implies the absorption of all differentiating qualities into the Godhead, the latter implies the preservation and perpetuation or creation of some new ones) – in one sense of the term God-realisation.[2] Thus we must distinguish within realised beings between those who still had some *karma* to work out (and were hence bound to the cycle of rebirth) and those (not only Self- but also God- realised) who had no more *karma* left to discharge (and were so not bound to the cycle, but could freely choose to manifest in particular circumstances). Self-realisation of the individual took two forms. As specified by the *Gita*, it involved a yoga of renunciation, a dialectic of inaction and a yoga of action, or a dialectic of action. Success in the

2 The other sense of God-realisation is as 'unity existence' or universal self-realisation.

former inevitably helped the latter and, in a full-blown dialectic of absolute and relative, of inner and outer fulfilment, success in the latter (through negentropic, spontaneous right action) eased the way for success in the former. However the dialectic of action was not only immediately compassionate but also implied a commitment to compassionate action (through some or other variant of the dialectic of desire to freedom). In this respect it was maximally evolutionary and maximally beneficial for both self and others. However, in the end the only resolution of social ills, the cause of all alienation, (including the alienations produced as an effect of structural sins) was the de-alienation of individuals from their true selves. And so all truly compassionate action was directed to, or at least conjoined with, a conatus to the self-realisation (becoming or realisation of what they already essentially were), true liberation or emancipation of the agents or agents concerned. And by a short route this implied that only universal self-realisation would satisfy the demands of compassion, or the logic of the desire for freedom or of that of solidarity in the abolition of structural sins implicit in spontaneous right action, or the God-like dharmic standpoint from which it occurred. Individual self-realisation thus entailed a conatus to universal self-realisation. But by the same token, given the interconnectedness, the holistic quality of social life on the physical plane, or while karmic relations remained, individual self-realisation was logically incomplete without universal self-realisation. Thus the Vedic formula 'I am the Totality' took on a new and sharper meaning.

The dialectics of inaction – of ontological access (in both its meditational and gracious forms), of shedding or purification, of embodiment and of witnessing – and the dialectics of action – of praxis, of the desire for freedom, of compassion or solidarity in totalising and collective agency (and of philosophical recapitulation) – were all intimately connected. Individual self-realisation entailed social change, which it encouraged; and social change, including political transformation, paved the way (for example, through educational and associated reforms) for individual self-realisation. The project of universal self-realisation was thus implicit in every moment of the spiritual life. Its actuality is God-realisation in the second sense of that term: 'unity existence'. This led L11 to see that, alongside his development and systematisation of dialectics of inaction, he must come to a greater understanding of the contours of social life. While each society would be a concrete universal (or rather consist of many such) in its own right, there must be some general features common to all of them. So L11 began to sketch out the basic features of what I have called four-planar social being: social transformation would take place under the dominance of transformation at pole (d), the stratification of the concretely singularised self. All change began here. However, though the process of self-realisation would subtly and directly affect other selves, it in no way abolished the need for – rather it logically entailed – action at the other poles of social being: namely (a) our material transactions with nature, (b) our interpersonal transactions and (c) social structure itself and in particular against the various dimensions of structural – and we can add ecological – sin.

All action indeed began with the self. But there were two directions of self-expansion: a vertical dimension towards unity with the *Atman* or soul, with the God-stuff which once achieved constituted a culmination of the process of self-realisation (this was the direction of the dialectics of inaction) and then there was the horizontal direction of self-expansion as the principle of subject or self-referentiality was extended to others and our productions (for example, social structures) and even the natural world itself (this was the direction of the dialectics of action). A renowned teacher of yoga (on which more anon), L11 was quick to see that the Vedic and indeed Eastern emphasis had been on the vertical direction of self-expansion, that is from self to Self or from self to Self as soul, that is as the (individuated) manifestation of God-stuff or spirit. This needed to be complemented by the Western emphasis on the horizontal direction of self-expansion (which may of course have subtle resonances and aeffects, reflections, generalisations and analogues at non-physical planes of being, possibly with their own subsequent physical effects), that is from self to Totality. Logically, this second direction could only be completed when all the components of the totality and the totality itself were realised. Then the second direction would be to Self as spirit as Totality, that is to universal self-realisation (or the realisation of all individuals or beings in that totality and of the totality itself). The primacy of (d) was thus apparent at the beginning as well as the end of the exercise.[3] But L11 was astute enough to realise that the totalising move was a strength and genuine contribution of the Western approach. It was ultimately defective insofar as it could not be achieved without individual self-realisation and that entailed praxis oriented to the project of universal self-realisation, but it at least gestured in this direction. For too long the Eastern world had been obsessed with projects of often ill-founded personal salvation to the neglect of social ills. What was happening in India now was in effect the *karma* of this neglect. L11 would set out to repair it.[4] Therefore he undertook to dialectically (concretely) universalise and make universally accessible his philosophy. To this end he wrote in English, travelled to England and elsewhere in the West and began a study of social movements and transformations to complement his earlier study of religious and political systems. It is this project that would be carried out in L12–L15 in experiencing and then mapping the contours of the socio-economic world.

But in L11 he was faced with two contradictions. On the one hand that, apart

3 Thus also the truth of the inversion of the Vedic formula: 'the Totality is I'.

4 And with it the (in Hegelian terms) *unhappy consciousness* of humanity, split between this-worldly (immanent, relative-oriented) West and other-worldly (transcendental, absolute-besotted) East.

from preaching a doctrine of active *ahimsa* or non-violence (as a social counterpart to the dialectics of inaction), in an early anticipation of Gandhianism, there was little that he could do in India, wrought as it was by the effects of successive invasions and the growing power of British rule and commercial capitalism. Second, he was in a theory–practice contradiction of his own. He had spent so many of his immediately previous lives in dialectics of inaction, on the path of renunciation, following the way of the recluse that, despite his tantric practices and his rigorous meditations focused on the activation of all the *chakras*, he was basically in (if not out of) his head. His own dialectic of embodiment was incomplete. His next life would thus have to be lived under the sway of the base *chakra*. And he would have to struggle in L13–L14 to make his way up through the *chakras* again. Similarly, his own movement was unrooted, being dependent on the largesse of princes and proto-industrialists and interested Westerners: a largesse that was readily forthcoming, it must be said, and helped him maintain his huge entourage. So he would have to come to terms with the world of wealth and poverty again, experiencing, then understanding it. Money, someone had said, was the lowest form of God-consciousness, but it was however a necessary and increasingly universal means of exchange and accumulation of energy. More generally, he would have to experience and understand power in all its secular varieties. All this implied that his soul must take the turn from the path of renunciation to the path of action, from the way of the recluse to the way of the householder. It implied that the ashrams must be dispersed and rebuilt in the heart of every human being and in the context of day-to-day activities in the relative world, a partial return to the 'middle truth' (albeit in a much more mediated and dialectical way). Then L9 taught that one could find emptiness anywhere; now he (and we) must find it everywhere – subjectively, from the standpoint of 'unity consciousness' oriented to the objective and absolute goal of universal self-realisation – in which the free development of each would be a condition, as Marx was to put it, of the free development of all. To change the world, to reorient it to this project, he would also have to change himself. The recluse would have to become a householder; the saint become a sexual being; the intellect walk as well as talk; the heart re-experience suffering as well as bliss.

A huge figure, L11 helped to prepare the ground for the renaissance of Vedic philosophy in the nineteenth century. He believed that the powers of man were only in their infancy. And he readily encouraged his followers in the practice of refined levels of perception and activity. Miracles, he argued, certainly occurred, and could in principle be effected by anyone, *qua* substrate of absolute powers; similarly with clairvoyance. Much could be achieved by a re-excavation of the logic of *ritambhara*, as originally (at least in recorded history) expounded by Patanjali in his *Yoga Sutras*. This involves activity on the threshold of the absolute or the non-dual state of experience (the state of emptiness or self-transcendence or bliss); techniques of *sanyama* or coherence, the holding together – or co-presence – of this state with the dualistic state of perception and activity in the relative world; that is, techniques for developing consciousness on the threshold of the absolute, techniques which made possible the realisation of all manner of things. It was from this level that spontaneous right action occurred, and it was at this level that the enlightened or truly realised man lived every moment of his being.

A charismatic figure, with long hair and a face of sweet innocence, he was not only a profound thinker but a man of, if not always in, the world. Criss-crossing India with his entourage, or sitting in his ashram surrounded by members of his retinue or followers, who he was quick to scold but equally quick to forgive, many apocryphal stories surround him. Thus it is said that when he was sitting meditating one day Krishna appeared beside him and garlanded a white cow with roses, and as Krishna took out his flute a magical lotus-strewn lake appeared in front of them and then all around them and they spent the whole night long in this way in blissful reverie. On another occasion, it is said, he was sitting meditating clad only in a loincloth when a female devotee (B) went down on his clearly visible erect lingham and brought him to orgasm without disturbing his equanimity or repose in the absolute at all. A mild rebuke to the devotee was all that followed the next day. At his funeral, hundreds of thousands lined the streets, and there were banner headlines around the world, in Paris, Rome, New York and London. Our soul was moving West.

8

BACK TO BASICS: LIFE AS A SULTAN AND ITS *KARMA*

Life Twelve: The Sufi sultan

We have seen that it is necessary for the soul last incarnated as L11, in order to complete the formulation of the project of universal self-realisation in its totalising, horizontal or Western direction of orientation,[1] to come to terms with the world of wealth and power, sexuality and money and the boundaries that delineate the physical world from which he has become so detached. He is thus born into a royal family in the Arabian peninsula (not far from Bahrain) and destined to become a sultan. As such, he spends his days alternating between the pleasures of life in his harem with his twenty-eight wives/concubines – one for each day of the lunar cycle – and of his innumerable horses or racing camels. In fact, his harem is more extensive than this; twenty-eight is just the official count. Many of its members are incarnations of souls that he has had outstanding karmic relations with in previous lives, sometimes in role-reversed positions. At any rate, riding horses and the pleasures of intercourse are the main preoccupations of his life in his later youth and early adulthood. Indeed, he cannot make up his mind between them. Love of Self identified as feeling good in bodily (and socially empowered) self is expressed in an equivocation between love of women and love of horses. Camels are a distinct third down the line. Later, this equivocation or ambiguity will express itself as a conflict between love of God and love of women, the expression of a more direct conflict between Self and self. He is also concerned with power, dispensing arbitrary or calculated justice throughout his land, and money, counting his treasure chest, replete with gold and laced with glittering rubies, emeralds and diamonds several times a week. It grows, as does his land and his power, as do his women and his male slaves, whom he treats alike as means to his ends.

1 It is worth re-emphasising that work at (d) – and is not all work *at* (d), irrespective of its object, i.e. whether it is *on* (a), (b), (c) – (or for that matter (d)) will already have emergent holistic effects, including possible aeffects at non-physical planes of being carried by subtler than physical energies.

Yet, as he ages, his spiritual side, always present, begins to develop within him, and under the tuition of a Sufi master, he comes to adore something higher than himself. The veil ceases to become the threshold for sexual pleasure and becomes a simple covering of the transcendence of God. He would like to discover God in himself, as he slowly uncovers his more feminine side (the woman *in* himself as distinct from the woman *for* himself). He learns the techniques of Sufi meditation, chanting in invocation the or a name of God. One night when dreaming, he sees himself as a small child not far away in Palestine, back in L1, breaking a bowl of water and being consoled by his kindly father (Fg). Oh, how he longs for such consolation of his soul now. Oh, how he longs for the purity the water both symbolises and brings. He is living in a material oasis, but he recognises himself as subsisting in a spiritual desert. As he awakens, he finds himself magically initiated into the mysteries of being. Nothing outwardly much has changed, but inwardly he has touched Self. He has been graced by access to his soul – the feminine principle (in Sufi Islam), though actually it both contains and is beyond both/all sexes – the principle that he had sought in women, in a displacement of his Self. He will now place a rose in his room every night as a symbol of his desire for that union with his higher self which in some way reflects the glory of God. As he grows older he develops a fondness, indeed a craving for music and dancing, and in his favourite dancer he begins to find the magic of a new, different kind of transcendence as his *kundalini* energy starts to flow upwards again. He continues his reading and dancing with the Sufi poets and musicians. Pious now, he begins to radiate a different kind of spirit before he dies. He wishes to see the world unified in the spirit of joy and justice.

What is the meaning of the life? Each life satisfies a desire or fills an incompleteness or lack experienced in some previous life (in accordance with the *karma* sown in previous lives). This life has a triple function: it begins the journey west; it is part of a dialectic of embodiment, to earth, root or ground the soul's experience; and it is a part of the project of understanding the co-ordinates of the socio-economic/political world necessary to complete the horizontal direction of self-expansion in L11's formulation of his project, of *the* project rather, of universal self-realisation, which is the *dharma* or vocation of the soul. The soul is not leading a very spiritual existence for much of this life, or so it would seem. However it is part of the truth of the 'middle truth' to see spirituality where it is not immediately apparent. The bedroom of L8 has become the harem of L12; the prostitute in L8 the sultan in L12. L8 will try to see the Buddha nature even in her oppressors. In this way she assuages the bitterness felt by her predecessor in L3, being able now to forgive and let go of the past. L2 knew many techniques of self-realisation, but only through the experiences of lives of service and discipline could he come, by L9–L11, to realise these techniques in practice, that is to embed them. The task of L12 is to shed the illusions of the recluse, whether in the form they took in L2, L9 or L11; to see spirituality as a practical affair and of practical concern to the ordinary man and woman. (I will have some more to say about shedding illusions in a moment.) It thus plays a vital part in the dialectic of embedding the absolute in the relative, by shedding illusions about personal salvation, theoretical knowledge and the possibility of an absolute way of being irrespective of the collective *karma* of humanity. The ashram is now in every person's living room, in every kitchen, bedroom, factory and shop; in every field, on the mountaintops and in the oceans as well. The dialectic of embodiment necessitates the spiritualisation of the totality of all of one's being and that logically entails the spiritualisation of the totality of the whole of manifest being. Self-realisation by an individual does not require universal self-realisation, but it implies and depends upon a *commitment* to it. But the nature of the indivisibility of totality must not be misunderstood. What is required is also (but only) that each and every being should shed a sub-totality, that sub-totality which consists of all its heteronomous orders of determination, those levels of constraint which make it something other than itself. So there is much in existence that must be shed and much to be positively absented or eliminated, to be fought against. Evil, including its manifestation as structural sin, exists and is rampant in the world of *maya* and *avidya*. This is the truth of the metaphor of life as a battle, in which the gods fight against the demons. The truth of the middle truth, of unity consciousness, is that the demons are entirely parasitic upon the gods. They exist only by virtue of their lack of self-realisation, so to speak. Heteronomous orders of determination are embedded within an autonomous whole. Man is essentially free, creative and Godlike, and the dialectic of shedding is dialectic of the shedding of the illusions which obscure that fact. This shedding has its own logic, which the dialectic of universal self-realisation aspires to empower and expedite.

Let me just briefly rehearse the contours of this dialectic of shedding.

1 To become full of God we have to shed the demons – the demons are the illusions (we have about the world, and especially ourselves) – ingrained dispositions which are habits, behaviours, constituting counter-conative $tendencies_2$,[2] excess baggage, heteronomous orders of determination, constraints on self-realisation.
2 So these illusions are practical affairs: that is, they underpin or constitute beliefs which inform desires and fears, which constitute habits, $tendencies_2$, patterns of behaviour which constitute excess baggage, heteronomous orders of determination, acting as constraints on self-realisation.

2 In the sense of tendency as a predisposition to behave that I introduced in *A Realist Theory of Science*, Appendix to Chapter 3.

3 And it requires transformed transformative practice to shed these illusions (the chains that metaphorically bind humans to live in Plato's cave), which are things like 'doing drugs, alcohol, sloth, lack of self-esteem, lack of compassion', to overcome all of which requires work on (d) and work at (d) on (a), (b), (c) and for that matter (d). (Habits produce self-justifying rationalisations, which interlock on to the initial set of illusory beliefs; for example, drugs will 'produce happiness'.)

4 Illusions are not soft; they are hard and require transform*ed* transformative praxis (see (3)).

5 Illusions inform vices, which typically take the form of two excesses (manifesting lack of mean or balance or correct measure, proportion, ratio). Thus, for example, under and over self-indulgence; that is lack of or excessive self-indulgence (in food, drink, sleep, pleasure and so on). For example one part of us – the self – wants to sleep; and another part – the Self – wants to get up to work. Then the self will think up a self-interested compromise: 'well, it's Sunday, I can afford to let myself spend an extra two hours in bed'.

6 To be enlightened – en-lightened – to know in the sense of know $_p$ is to know what you = yourSelf wants (to become enlightened is to have become what (and only (as in the dialectic of shedding) and fully (as in the dialectic of embodiment)) we ourselves are.

7 Sometimes you can use a tendency$_2$, such as a bodily disposition (or perhaps a feeling, in the heart or solar plexus centre) to play off, bribe or counteract another tendency$_2$ as ingrained in a behavioural routine. This is the Machiavellian (realpolitikal or 'cruel to be kind') moment in transformative work at (d).

Life Thirteen: Poverty in southern Italy (Amalfi) – the outcast

We have seen that L12 before he dies wishes to see the world unified in the spirit of joy and justice. But first the *karma* of this life must be played out. Born in southern Italy, near Amalfi, L13 is endowed with a huge mind but experiences a life of suffering, frustration and desire. His throat *chakra* is blocked and he is unable to express himself properly in his speech or in anything he does. He has no resources. Still, he is cheerful. With his peasant wife (MgL) he ekes out a meagre existence, seeing the rich and famous (some of them his former concubines and slaves) prosper at his and his like's expense. He dies young, a Sparticist.

What is the significance of this life? It clearly shows the opposite pole of the socio-economic world to L12. To understand this world, and to embed reason, freedom and spirituality within it (that is, to emancipate humanity from constraints), it is necessary to consider and experience it as a totality. One opposite swings into another. To understand the middle truth of a situation, it is necessary to see the absolute or autonomous being in that situation (from which all that is negative (normatively) or heteronomous derives its energy or light) and to see the role that that situation plays in the process of the self-realisation of that absolute or autonomous being in and through the relative world. Now to see that role entails accepting the situation just as it is; but accepting it in the present does not imply tolerating it for the future. Attention to and total acceptance of the present is a prerequisite for that present's intentional transformation in the future. Life is a process that cannot be frozen. And the process of self-realisation, on which we are all embarked, whether we know it or not, begins with a transformation in the transformative practices in which we are inevitably engaged;[3] the process is one of transform*ed* or rather transform*ing* transformative (totalising and trustworthy) practices. It is finally worth noting how the dialectic of shedding shows the way in which a totality can be both simpler (in virtue of being free from extraneous or heteronomous orders of determination) and yet complete. The life of unity existence may be both fuller, in the sense of more abundant, differentiated and rich in being and activity (being and activity which is at present blocked by heteronomous orders of constraint) and simpler, precisely in the sense that it is free of those extraneous determinations, those constraints inherited as the *karma*, legacy or presence of the past. To truly be in the moment is to be free of the presence of the past, to be attentive to the present (accepting and non-judgemental about it) and intentionally oriented to and for the future.

Life Fourteen: The French philosopher – the sceptical mystic

L13 sets the theme for a Western life of a better-off, but also of a distinctly amystical bent. We have already encountered L14. In fact, we are seeing everything from L2 on through and by courtesy of his time machine, and I will comment on this in a moment. A university professor and prolific writer, he is also a mystic in awe of nature (especially the stars; astrologically, not just astronomically), a doctor concerned with new ways of (self) healing, a political revolutionary who believes in the possibility of a society without money and one which would satisfy the ideals of primitive communism. Born of French diplomatic parents (near the Swiss border), he is educated in England, where they have been posted, by a stern governess from whom he quickly grows free. He travels widely, is fluent with languages and interested in all aspects of the revolutions of modernity. He travels to America and Russia, deriding both. He is a naturalist who believes in angels

3 See *The Possibility of Naturalism*, Chapter 2 for the 'transformational model of social activity'; see also *Dialectic: The Pulse of Freedom*, Chapter 2.9.

and fairies. He is both strongly intuitive and strongly intellectual; both an academic and a populist. (Thus in Russia he reports the revolution and its consequences for a French newspaper; while in America he preaches the need for social reform to a lay audience, with the New Testament by his side.) He cannot however synthesise these different aspects of his mind and personality. In particular he cannot integrate left and right brains, intellect and intuition, or as they are sometimes called, head and heart. In his intuitive capacity he is a supernaturalistic naturalist who is disposed to see the manifestations or presence of consciousness everywhere. In his intellectual capacity he swears by Kant, Hegel and Marx. In his right brain he has much in common with the Chinese philosopher of L9, whereas in his left brain he resembles the Ancient Greek one of L2, or the cardinal of L6. However, if the emphasis in L6 was on the left brain, the intellect, here it is at least balanced by recognition of the co-equal importance of the right brain, intuition. A famous professor, with a considerable following, and a mystic in love with nature (including human being), he cannot integrate the two sides of his existence. He cannot realise himself as a totality.

L12 had the power but not the disposition to be free, i.e. for self-realisation. L13 had the disposition but not the power for it. Both disposition and power are present in L14 but there is still something lacking. His heart has been opened; he has been to India, spending some time at Adyar near Madras at the headquarters of the Theosophical Society, and been much impressed by both the Ramakrishna Mission (founded by Swami Vivekananda) and the conversations he has had with Sri Aurobindo and Paramahansa Yogananda, from whom he had received instruction in meditative techniques. He has become interested, as we have seen, by the phenomena that can only be revealed by an opening third eye. But he remains split by the dichotomy between intuition and intellect, more precisely between what he can see (or practically knows) and what he can justify by reason. He begins to see his mission, to be completed in L15, to be that of a synthesis of East and West, spirituality and science, reason and intuition. The process of this completion will necessitate the systematic taking through of Western philosophy, and more generally Western social and political thought, to its critical limits and showing how it, taken to these limits, systematically undermines its own crude materialism and ushers in, indeed necessitates, a philosophy of Self-realisation. (See the general theoretical introduction in Part I.) At the same time, this theoretical synthesis must be given a practical form by being embedded in a heart and engaged in activity which has shed all attachment, which is truly free, and has let go of the past and all its encumbrances. And so the way is paved for L15.

9

THE DANCE OF SHIVA IN THE AGE OF AQUARIUS

Life Fifteen: The circle completed – from East to West – liberation or the path to enlightenment

This chapter will be brief, as the life it describes is as yet unfinished and there is much further work to be done. It represents however the fulfilment of the desire set off in L11 and rekindled in L14: the desire for transcendence to a greater (and complete) totality. Born in London in 1944 of an Indian father and an English mother, his task is to reconcile and resynthesise the opposites: East and West, male and female, *yin* and *yang*, reason and experience, fact and value, mind and body, heaven and earth, they aspectually embody. Abused as a young child, he suffers a miserable childhood, despite his theosophical upbringing. Finally he flees home with an Oxford scholarship to study philosophy, politics and economics, against his father's wishes. He gains honour after honour, but with each original twist in his life and thought he suffers the rejection of the system. He achieves all he sets himself. He eventually becomes as radical and revolutionary as it is possible to get in Western philosophical terms, until materialism is transcended in the context of a global philosophy, both perennially old and radically new; a perennial philosophy for the new millennium which this very book initiates. The means and end is enlightenment, and universal human emancipation is seen to be a condition of planetary survival. This philosophy also contains an integration of some of the insights of the New Age and the New Left movements.

L15 sees the integration of the *chakra* system, fulfilling the desire of L11 and realising the goal of L9 on the basis of the inspirations afforded by Jesus in L5, Moses in L1, Pythagoras in L2, Buddha in L10, Krishna in L11 and many others in life after life. As shown at the beginning, in the foreword, each life is connected with a different colour or *chakra*, or complex of colours or *chakras*. Each life is karmically connected to some life or lives preceding it and following it. The sequence of lives is completed only when the desire for desire, the cause of all suffering, is relinquished.

Let me elaborate a bit on the transformation of dialectical critical realism into the philosophy of self-realisation (and ultimately universal self-realisation) as outlined in the introduction to the book and in the general theoretical introduction in Part I, by once more thematising it in the context of the critique of Hegelian dialectic, with its platinum plate, golden nugget, mystical shell and rational kernel. The fundamental problem was revealed by analysis of the platinum plate. For this suggested that the irrealism of contemporary (and most hitherto existing) philosophy reflected an irrealist categorial structure of society, an irrealist society itself replete with reifications and alienations, real suffering and real oppression. In what sense, then, could realism claim to be true? It could only claim to be true if underlying this irreal categorial structure was a real deeper realist one which had been occluded and overlain by irrealism. And this leads naturally enough into the idea of the co-presence of real and irreal categorial structures and correspondingly of autonomous and heteronomous orders of determination. The chief mechanism of liberation (understood as social liberation) in *DPF*, namely the dialectic of desire for freedom, therefore had to be recast in the context of a more general dialectic of shedding or the disemergence of irrealist and heteronomous structures. In its new form, the dialectic of the desire for freedom could thus be further generalised. As is well known, it moves from a desire to the desire to understand and remove the causes of constraints which prevent the satisfaction of that desire and thence, by the inexorable logic of dialectical universalisibility, to a commitment on the part of the agent to remove all dialectically similar constraints and thence to the removal of all constraints as such in virtue of their dialectical similarity. The extension in *From East to West* sees the fundamental cause or constraint on human satisfaction or happiness (i.e. the failure to satisfy desires) as lying in desire or craving *itself*. This is not, however, the end of the matter, for desire as such is caused by *avidya* or ignorance of the true nature of man, manifest in attachment and man's alienation from himself and the totality he inhabits, and ultimately God. And the desire to end one's own suffering (alienation and state of desiring) – in self-realisation – itself entails, through the inexorable logic of dialectical universalisability (as manifest in the dialectic of desire for freedom), commitment to end the suffering of all dialectically similar beings, i.e. to the project of universal human self-realisation, and thence to end the suffering of all beings as such, in virtue of their dialectical unity as beings, i.e. to truly universal eudaimonia. The cause of all suffering, the ultimate constraint on human happiness, then, is our alienation from our true selves and from others, ultimately the rest of the cosmos: two forms of alienation from God. In a eudaimonistic society there would still be intentionality, but not desire or craving as such, with its self-undermining and repetitive character; intentionality would manifest itself in the free realisation of aims, goals and projects.

On this new conception, man is already and essentially enlightened. And man's goal in life is to become self-conscious of his enlightenment. This is something that must be learned rather than given, and is gradually acquired or revealed in the context of a learning process, which is essentially one of disemergence; the shedding of illusion or ignorance and the re-realisation of his true self. From this perspective, evil or ignorance is a sort of grand illusion which we must experience to become self-consciously aware of the true nature of ourselves as concretely singularised, unique God-stuff. The platinum plate and the golden nugget in the critical reception of Hegelian dialectic by dialectical critical realism thus come very much to the fore in this new transcendental turn within (or perhaps beyond) it.

But the mystical shell and the rational kernel remain important too. Ontological monovalence and the repression of absence mean that both incompleteness and creativity, therefore the driving force and the means of resolution of dialectical learning processes, become occluded. The result is reification, fixism and fatalism. In this new context, the rational kernel of Hegelian dialectic as a dialectical learning process is to underpin the ideas of reincarnation, *karma* and liberation. Another word for *karma* (besides action) is learning. And souls, in their sequence of lives, are placed, or place themselves, precisely in those learning situations which paradigmatically will optimally encourage or promote the soul's capacity to learn more about the true nature of itself and its environment, to strengthen its soul force and to encourage its development on the path to consciousness of itself (that is to Self-consciousness) in human life on earth.

Let me briefly review the schema which has been called MELD (1M to 4D) in the context of the philosophy of universal self-realisation which has been elaborated in this book. From 1M we have the idea of God as the ultimate categorial structure of the world and of the emergence and disemergence of ignorance, evil and structural sin. From 2E we have the bi-polar role of absence, as both the signal that something is wrong and, in the context of transcendence, the mechanism for putting it right. From 3L we have the necessity to overcome alienation in two dimensions: vertical, that is, alienation from Self in the (paradigmatically Eastern) project of individual Self-realisation; and in a horizontal direction paradigmatically alienation from community (the Western emphasis), but which can (and must) be extended, on the logic of the dialectic of the desire for freedom, to the project of universal self-realisation. From this new standpoint, totality and liberation amount to the same thing; or rather liberation, the goal of 4D, is just a human instantiation of totality (the goal of 3L) so that, just as what in *Plato Etc.* I called 5C (fifth component), namely the social field, can be inscribed within and deduced from the categorial structures of 4D, so the categorial structures of 4D can be inscribed within those of 3L, as a special case of them. Focusing specifically on 4D, however, we can see that the criterion of absolute reason or the unity of theory and practice in practice and the goal of reflexive consistency can only be satisfied by enlightenment. For any attachment or self-alienation will result in error and generate the possibility of theory/practice inconsistency. Indeed, error, the product of incompleteness (here alienation of man from himself), must result in contradiction and split, a contradiction and split which will pull thought and deed, theory and practice (at some level, in some respect) apart.

I will conclude this reconsideration of the theme of the introduction to the book by noting the significance in this new context of the four existing benchmarks in the development of dialectical critical realism. Transcendental realism, establishing the stratification and differentiation, including emergence and transfactuality of being, establishes the necessity for ontology and for the dispositional and categorial realisms developed in section 1 of the general theoretical introduction. Critical naturalism, oriented to the overcoming of dualisms, establishes the goal of de-alienated man in his totality; and the theory of explanatory critique tells us to seek this goal in reality itself (values do not subsist in a realm apart from it). The process of man's liberation for its part is dialectical. Learning is essentially creative as is all truly human practice and each act of creativity comes *ex nihilo*, in mimetic reproduction of God's creation of the universe. This is the significance of the realism about transcendence articulated here. We are in essence already gods; and to realise this we only have to become what we already essentially are. To reclaim reality, we must first reclaim ourselves.

Let me sum up the main thesis of the book. Man is essentially free and essentially God (therefore essentially one, but as a unity-in-diversity and as concretely singularised therefore also essentially unique). Man is essentially creative and essentially being (subject-referential) as opposed to having (attached, object-referential) and essentially embodied, engaged in, intentional but unattached activity; man is essentially enlightened not ignorant (avidyic); man is essentially dharmic rather than karmic; human action is essentially spontaneous right action, which is carefree, joyous and loving and which needs no justification or additional thought, not erroneous, mediated or doubtful, not evil, sinful or constraining; and man is essentially autonomous not heteronomous. To realise these truths, all man has to do is to shed his illusions and to let go of the past and the heteronomous orders of determination which constrain, check and otherwise thwart him. Such illusions, orders and constraints have arisen as emergent products of man's free will. As his nature has been occluded, he needs also a dialectic of access; and as his energy has been blocked, he needs also a dialectic of embodiment. To get these dialectics working, he needs to witness his activity. As the dialectics of inaction are perfected and he sheds his past and embeds his real essence more fully in his life, he will act more and more mindfully, in the moment and spontaneously rightly. As his action becomes more spontaneously right it will become more coherent, creative, aefficacious and compassionate. Any residual desire or attachment will set in motion a dialectic of desire for freedom in which the desire for attachment gives way to the desire for enlightenment (or the state of desirelessness) and this ushers in, bolstered by dialectics of love, compassion and solidarity, involving collective and totalising activity, as well as philosophical recapitulation of the past,[1] the project of universal self-realisation. To this, each human being is in every act logically committed. To change the world, man only has to realise himself. This is a dream that many radicals, including Rousseau and Marx, have had, namely that man to be free has only to throw off the shackles of constraint that inhibit the realisation of his true being and which underpin, as conditions of their possibility, the emergence of those constraints. Surprisingly enough this is a vision which conforms entirely with the system of Vedantic philosophy that comes down to us from ancient India. Man to be free has only to shed his illusions, the world of *avidya* or *maya* that is an emergent, false but real, product of his activity in the relative phase of existence. If man is essentially free, both radical West and mystical East can unite in agreeing that the goal of life is to re-realise this essential freedom, to become what we essentially are and have never ceased to be, despite all our illusions to the contrary. To become free all we need to do is to shed our illusions. These are the chains which bind us to the presence of the past. It is time to let go, to live life afresh. The hour for unconditional love has struck.

1 Thus modern philosophy begins with the Cartesian ego. Kant sees this to be an impossibility, and argues that an objective manifold is a condition of the possibility of the subjective transcendental unity of perception, which reciprocally allows us to synthesise the empirical manifold presented by a world unknowable in itself. Hegel sees the transcendental unity of self-consciousness as a social achievement which is ultimately grounded in a public world of moral order, enshrined in the constitutional structures of his rational state. But Marx identifies the real basis of the Hegelian state in civil society founded on the alienation, exploitation and suffering of man. The further transcendental turn is to see this suffering and that oppression as grounded in structures of *avidya* and *maya*, of self-alienation of humanity. These structures of self-alienation and ignorance, these real illusions and that real suffering and oppression are however entirely parasitic on the essential freedom (enlightenment) and creativity of man, in which consideration lies the permanent possibility of its overthrow. Man's enlightenment pre-exists and post-exists his suffering and ignorance, but he becomes Self conscious and realised (actualised and experienced in practice, on the physical plane) as a result of overthrowing the veils which are there precisely for that very purpose.

INDEX